Letters

to

Lightworkers

Letters

to

Lightworkers

Diane Hall
& Peter Elohim

Letters to Lightworkers

©Diane Hall 2011

ISBN: 978-1-3262792-6-4

www.dianehallsbooks.co

To lightworkers everywhere: sleeping, awakening or wandering through a dream in discomfort, ready to shed your human skin, spread your angelic wings and shine your light...so others might also come to know them selves as Angels... Namaste.

Dear Lightworkers, Yes YOU!!!

For those of you who are not already familiar with this work, I'll just explain, briefly, how it came into being and then I'll leave you to enjoy it at your leisure.

The articles in the first half of this book were created for members of Evolving Consciousness, a Facebook group I created in the late summer of 2008 for the purpose of sharing insights, musings and channelling regarding how we might all remain inspired, grounded and positive during this time of incredible transformation on Earth. Since I began writing these messages, I have been very moved by the lovely responses they have received and by knowing that they have made a difference to so many light-workers and consciously evolving souls on a committed path of spiritual growth and awakening.

The pace of our awakening and the changes taking place in our world are sometimes exhausting for us to process and, at the same time, with enough understanding of their meaning, they are also awe-inspiringly hopeful. As always, there are two stories running parallel to each other. There is, even at the eleventh hour, a dualistic free-will offering laid out before us: on the one hand, taunting us with a dubious timeline, which stretches forth from a questionable past, and on the other, tantalising us with a golden, utopian future. This book offers an opportunity to explore the more positive possibilities while not once forgetting where we have evolved from, and to look ourselves in the eye regarding a few choice questions about how we want shape the world for our children and yes, it IS time for us to decide, without a doubt.

In fact, it's probably more accurate to say that we have already made our choice on many unseen and often unperceived levels of experience and only have to look around us at the incredible break-throughs in thought, consciousness and possibility to see evidence of this. But as with many major Earthly manifestations at this current level of density, matter is taking its time to catch up with imagination.

Nevertheless, there is a rapid quickening, and the utopian intentions and petitions of the crowds of light-workers currently shaking things up on this lethargic landmass will eventually come to fruition as our ascension into increasingly finer frequencies leads us inevitably towards a lighter consciousness and an exciting range of consistently lighter choices in thought, word and deed.

After a long break from writing these messages, due to some, all-consuming, life-changing travel commitments, I recently returned with a new 5th dimensional blog and some further offerings of love and enlightened questioning. My hope is that all of these messages as a combined work will bring peace, hope and sometimes celebration as we seek to create the world as we would now choose to dream it and venture into a frequency that matches our dawning creation.

However, there is now also a new and exciting addition to my offerings. In the first section of the book, you will find a series of our usual messages in the format you might have grown used to, if you are familiar with our work. There is also the occasional sprinkling of poetry, and a few of those inspired, poetic phrases we sometimes create, as a quiet meditation, an encoded means of raising your vibration to the level of love, stillness or communion with all that is.

I love the idea that you can now have all of these articles and essays as one collection and find it even more exciting that you'll also now be able to have access to them in the form of a paperback book.

These messages are sometimes inspired or abetted by mediumistic input, sometimes partly channelled and sometimes just a bit of an indignant, indigo rant. However, for the first time, in the second half of the book, I would like to hand over the pages to my precious and beautiful Guide, Peter Elohim, who has been wishing, for some time now, to communicate with you directly, using me as a channel.

You might have realised by now that I often feel that there is so much to say and there barely seems enough time in which to say it all, hence the collection of novels... at least one of which, will be published very soon, after a really, truly, final revision over the Summer, once I get that virgo-licious sense of perfectionism to finally LET GO!!

I am not a perfected being by any means. At times I behave like a very limited and scared being... but I'm also a lot of fun, I'm told... when I really forget myself. At times, I am called to reach for the stars and I faithfully follow, regardless of the sacrifices. This is when we are at our best. More often than not, although I am fairly intelligent... I think... I am constantly learning, even as I write, from a far purer and more aligned intelligence as I sit at my laptop, shaking my head, sometimes crying and revelling in the revelations. Nevertheless, he insists that we are one and that all that he is, I AM and all that I AM, YOU ARE! And so I let go of definitions regarding how we work or what to call myself. I am not a channel. I AM that I AM. Everything and nothing and like you, with a world of change at my fingertips which I now lovingly embrace.

For a very long time, my collaboration with Peter has been a source of deep, deep personal joy. At the same time, I love to work as a writer as much as I love to work as a channel and I view both of these aspects of communication as my Divine purpose and absolutely feel, hear and revel in his contribution both to my inspired fictional writing and to these articles, musings and inspirations. For me, there is no more joyful occupation than work that involves his input. And so, we work together in this rapturous and sometimes indefinable way, celebrating our love of God in all his/her/it's many expressions, in order to bring a complete picture of the challenges inherent in communication between dimensions as well as the joys of experiencing such connections. In this way, we endlessly find ourselves exploring the interface between the human story and that of a far more ascended consciousness. It is... all of it... a part of who we are and what we agreed to convey and contribute in this lifetime. It illustrates our story perfectly, as we wrestle through the quirky, muddy waters of human thought, experience and emotion to reach for higher ground.

We are happy to deliver to you again and again, through our great, great love, what appears to be a glimpse of how this ascension operation feels, through story, supposition, sharing, splitting and at times completely submerging ourselves into the experience of how it feels to be human, how it feels to be ascended and how if feels to be at that crossroads where all worlds meet, collide, embrace and create a new piece of splendour that you might know as art.

However you wish to view us... he, me, it, we, you or they...know that we are one and that this oneness is also, in part, what we are currently expressing as we fuse our hearts, minds and souls to varying degrees at different times in order to illustrate and embody our purpose.

Do not seek to understand it with your minds... simply enjoy the sound and the feel and the joy of it.
I feel honoured that you have chosen to share my journey as I continue on my mission to bring these messages of love, light, personal and planetary transformation and Divine, loving service, out into the wider world.

Whoever you are and whatever your reason for reading this book, I hope it brings you as much joy as I have found in writing this selection of messages and compiling it.

Wishing you Loving, Angelic Light,

The Wisdom of The Buddhas

and The joy of a Fiery-hearted devotion to your God

Diane

We Are One

I turn away to find you once again

I let you go so I can truly hold you in my heart

I close my eyes so I might see you clearly

Surround myself with noise to shut out your voice,

Only to hear it once again in searching through the silent pain

You are the God within; you are the inner smile

You are the gentle stream that finds the ocean

I am as nothing but the shifting sands

And I am this, and that, and all, and one

While you are everything, and all, and none

Misunderstand you so that we might know you

Forget you so that we might soon recall

And hold you at a distance to embrace you

As many, in two minds, with one accord

Through freedom, do we find that you contain us

In satisfaction is our longing clear

Not one new thing have ever we begun

And as we lose ourselves, so are we won

Yes, as we lose ourselves, so ...we are one

Smiling at Life, The Universe and the Rollercoaster

It's been a strange week. So many people I have spoken to this week have told me what an intense time they've been having and how much seems to be changing in their lives. We are living in intense times; there's a lot of it about, perhaps; and perhaps there's also a lot of wonderful opportunity around us that we are not yet seeing or allowing ourselves to bring fully into focus.

After all, haven't we always been living in intense times? Haven't we also, always been living in incredible times in which we stand on the threshold of unprecedented potential for the growth and expansion of the human spirit into embodied higher consciousness? And haven't we always been the ones who are to make a choice about whether or not to embrace this? It feels challenging sometimes to always hold to the most positive dream we could conceive of right now in this moment when so much of what we see around us seems to threaten to pull us under into other, less resourceful ways of thinking and being in the world. And yet, it is at these very times when we must go inside ourselves and defiantly find a way to smile once again, the kind of smile which adds to the groundswell of consciousness awakening on our planet right now and affirms once again; "this is who I truly am. I am a joyous being who touches others with my joyful nature and adds my faithful presence to the mighty all and all which wishes to bring light, love and peaceful transformation here, right now.

I have also been feeling a momentous shifting, cleansing and challenging this week and an impulse to once again go beyond yet another barrier of fear in order to fulfil my dreams in all areas of life. In fact, it seems almost daily now that I am being asked, or guided, to do something which thrusts me squarely and unceremoniously outside of my comfort zone in order to create more happiness, peace, love and to make those dreams a reality. We all go through our ups and downs and have to sometimes embrace times of great questioning and events which challenge us to call upon our inner resources and find courage and resilience within ourselves, of which we were previously unaware.

It almost seems, in fact, that at this current time in our awakening as conscious spiritual beings in human form, we are faced with many changes and challenges both personally and globally. These changes are urging us to look within and begin awakening to ourselves and all that we can become, as we increasingly find that there is, indeed, nowhere else to turn if we wish to become peaceful.

This is the great journey of life and the wonder of its endless ability to bring us closer to ourselves, to each other and to the truth of who we are as magnificent creative beings able to choose our own reality. Sometimes it is exactly at times when we are pushed into these seemingly tortuous "happenings" that we find our greatest power to transform ourselves into another kind of being; a being who is capable of tremendous creativity, compassion, wisdom and an increased ability to create exactly the circumstances we wish to see in our lives. We realise on some level that we may have created these unfortunate circumstances for our own evolution and awakening and that we can just as easily turn the tide and begin to make choices which truly support and enrich who we are now becoming.

Sure it's easy to say that this is the case, and knowing it certainly doesn't mean that you wake up every single day full of beans, ready to take on the world, laughing hysterically at the joyous place in which you now find yourself to be. No! If that were the case we would never understand how truly blessed we are in those moments when all of the universe does, indeed, seem to conspire to bring us happiness and a sense of rightness in our choices. We all have times when we are learning something that feels tough to learn and we feel like just rubbing out last week and starting again.

However, as long as we have a sense that our overall movement is forward, and we are gradually increasing our ability to stay in this place of light and lightness for more sustained periods of time, then we are undoubtedly moving steadily towards the fulfilment of our dreams and increasing self-awareness and are very much on the right path.

We are multifaceted creatures of apparent duality, embracing a universe of contrast and infinite possibility, and, perhaps, all we can really do is to choose to follow our inner light and the dreams which burn brightly from within, keeping the flame alive and well in our hearts. Each moment of our lives we are faced with a choice as to whether we will continue to embrace the drama, the interest and the fascination which makes life on earth so different from that heavenly state of oneness and perfected awareness to which we will eventually return.

We can choose at any moment to expect, embrace and focus on the "peace we seek to become" or we can look at the many things which are wrong with our lives or not quite right about ourselves. We can grumble at and berate our selves for the silly mistakes we made that day, the wrong choices, the inane comments and the poor associations we once again allowed to mar our lives, or we can see ourselves as endlessly loving creative beings on a grand journey of self-discovery.

So what, so we didn't get everything right this week, this month, this year and we're certainly not where we expected to be at the beginning of the year and "hey what about all that law of attraction stuff; why isn't that working?" The fact is that we often set goals, create expectations and set ourselves up for disappointment by choosing not with our hearts but with our heads. And there is no peace to be found in the head. The heart holds the secrets of our true essential nature and therefore knows what will truly make us happy. When we begin to let go of the fear of what will happen if we give our heads a break, we will once again hear and follow the heart's wisdom and begin to become true co-creators with the infinite source of all love within the universe. For love is the only true creative impulse for all things which bring true joy.

Therefore let us be more gentle with ourselves; love ourselves as we would want another to love us; care for ourselves as we care for others and see through the illusion and the drama into the ever-present possibility that we are all that we need to be right now in this very moment. When we allow ourselves a moment or two to be still and to listen, in the very next instant, the heart runs to meet us, bringing to us its precious messages and drawing us once again into a smiling consciousness where we realise that we are so, so very blessed to live the lives we live, enjoy the smiles of those we love and have food in our stomachs, shelter over our heads and the fire in our souls which makes us wish for even more.

If a child falls while playing, you pick them up, dust them off and tell them gently and lovingly that it's just what happens sometimes, it's still okay to go back out to play. It isn't necessary that they stay at home forever now just in case they ever fall over and get hurt again. Your intention is to heal them; to quickly bring them back to their playful nature; to soothe and comfort them and to allow them to be themselves without fear and without the illusion or the grand expectation that life should always be perfect in every minute. You want them to learn that in the next moment all pain can be healed and turned into a more positive learning, and that you are there for them equally when they are in pain and when they are in joy. You love to see them happy and you love to see how strong they are becoming as they face life; with both its joys and its challenges, easily and effortlessly and without attachment to either.

Likewise, all of our emotional scrapes and bumps are just a part of life, and life is still a beautiful game despite the scratches and scars. Life can, indeed, at times, be a like an emotional roller-coaster and the only thing that changes our experience of this glorious ebbing and flowing; this wild round of uncertainty, change and blessed transformation and the inherent possibilities existent within the human condition, is, in fact, our perception of them. So whether we choose to abhor, to embrace, to deny or to dispense with the drama entirely; whether we chose to embrace change and to revel in the new discovery of what we might become or to simply hide away in fear, we may as well enjoy the ride.

The Truth about 2012

A friend asked me this week what I thought about 2012 and whether I believed that there's going to be a massive energy shift and a global re-awakening in consciousness at this time. Almost as soon as I began to reply, I felt the answer dawning on me from elsewhere, as the gentle rain of inspiration, once again, began to settle upon my heart and mind like those blessed drops of love, falling from the heavens.

Yes, there will be a massive shift in consciousness and, yes, the evidence is clear that we are already in the midst of it. However, we need to stop putting our energy into, once again, imagining that there is some specific date on which "something" "happens" which is somehow, sudden, surprising, new and bewilderingly outside of our collective consciousness and control.

Yes we are already in the midst of great change and, yes, we are indeed, currently, already witnessing the dawning of a new and glorious age in the consciousness and evolution of humanity, and it is something that WE are doing...it is not being done TO us and neither is it waiting to leap out at us at any particular prescribed moment. It is already within, without and all around about us!!

Neither is it some new and surprising thing, for there is, indeed, nothing new under the sun, and what we are in fact in the midst of, is simply a returning to the blissful state of that which we already, truly are. My guide describes the wonderful times we are now living through as a kind of birthing PROCESS in which we are bringing into fruition this wonderful new time about which we so often speculate.

When a mother is expecting a child, she is already a mother long before the birth of that child. Yes, even before that child comes into being, if she is even minutely perceptive, she will, on some subtle, vibrational and emotional levels, already have an awareness of its being and its holistic spiritual essence... and SUCH is the very nature of our current times. We sense great change all around us and have an inkling of an essence of an idea of what this wonderful time holds for us and yet, in truth, it us not until we truly hold that baby in our loving arms that we will begin to understand its awesome potential, its breath-taking beauty and its inexplicable ability to move us to great and courageous acts of selfless love and kindness.

Throughout the gestation period, the mother might be only vaguely aware of her ability to shape and to influence the nature of her child with what she puts into her body and what she allows into her mind; the thoughts she chooses to think and the loving intention she chooses to send in the direction of the beloved, growing foetus, through feelings, foods, moods and music. When that child is born, whether it arrives on time or slightly before or after the date circled on the calendar, the mother knows that the birth is not an end, not some inevitable target which she has been aiming to reach and which now heralds the end of all waiting, wondering, hoping and strife. She knows that, in fact, what she holds gently in her arms is just another beautiful beginning and that it is, now, certainly, in part at least, her words, her thoughts, her nurturing and the very same loving intent which created that wonderful being, which must now begin to shape and influence his or her destiny so that in time they might become a wonderful being of light and a vehicle for Divine inspiration which will transform lives, touch hearts and reaffirm, once again that, through love, all things are, indeed, possible, even the awakening of the most stubborn mind and the soothing of the most hardened heart.

There is never a point within this process when the enlightened mother says "Ooh, I'm loving this vodka and these cigarettes. Oooooh, I wonder what sort of kid I'll get? Oh, who cares, I only half believe it's coming anyway. Chances are, soon as it's born, I'll probably just cast it out into the world and see what happens. Oh who knows what'll happen when it's born, I certainly don't. I'm not a fortune-teller. No one can actually really know, anyway, can they?!!!" She knows, just as we now know, that the future is within the hands of those who are brave enough to dream of a better time and to take this dream, hold fast to it and nurture it with all our hearts, souls, minds and every iota of our ever-evolving consciousness, until it comes fully into being.

So, what *is* the truth about 2012? Well the truth is simply that there is no simple truth about this or about anything else. The truth is, as always, a moment of realisation waiting to be created, discovered and rediscovered anew and even one second after it is discovered, waiting to become a trivial nugget which is subject to scrutiny and altered by our ever-changing perceptions. Therefore, like everything else and every other possibility which exists in our lives and within our many worlds 2012 can either signal the dawn of a new time of peace, love, joy and blissful soul level consciousness on earth or it can signal a time of continued apathy, control, restriction and disappointment as we wait quietly and wonder what will happen next. Which one of these truths do you truly choose?

The choice has been ever-present at many junctures throughout time. It was there at the time of The Christ, it was there during the renaissance in Europe, it was there in 1967, it is here, now, in 2008 and it will still be with us in 2012. It is indeed always just a thought and a choice away.....

Love, Light and Blessings to all

Down the Rabbit Hole

Some years ago, I felt inspired to buy the film 'The Matrix.' I knew that there was something in it that would be significant to me but was, perhaps, on some other level of awareness, unready to receive it. So, I bought the film as a birthday gift for my brother.

Some time later, he thanked me for the film and said that it had gone into his top five movies of all time and was possibly, even, number 1. He then asked me what I thought of it, didn't I think it was amazing!? I confessed, somewhat sheepishly, that I hadn't actually seen the film, myself, because it just looked a bit boys- sci-fi-nerdy-action-flickish and not my sort of thing, exactly. But I gave it to him because I felt so powerfully guided to buy it.

"You have to see it..." was all he said.

Well, eventually, I did see it and it was almost a life-changing experience as I began to realise two things:

1 everything I believe about becoming completely empowered through altered, awakened consciousness, self-belief and self-mastery is true, despite some of the 'other' indications of our times, and...

2 lots of other people out there know it... AND this knowledge is growing, spreading and taking root... everywhere!!

For me this was before the halcyon days of "The Secret" and "What the Bleep..." and even though the messages in The Matrix were highly decorated with an accessible action-packed, shoot-'em-up Hollywood narrative, it was nevertheless a powerful tribute to the indomitable nature of the human spirit.

Recently, during a conversation with a wonderful friend, he told me the story of how, at some point in his life, he would watch this film and, time after time, would find himself just blacking out and going into a deep sleep whenever he got to the point in the film where Neo was given the choice as to whether to take the red pill or the blue. Once again this only serves to convince me that this is a very powerful film and a masterful celebration of spiritual insurrection.

But just what is it that's so powerful about it and what is it that so many of us initially fear about taking that little red pill? What is it that makes us cling to "The world that has been pulled over your eyes to blind you from the truth"? Well, for one thing, we know within our hearts, that to 'take the red pill', is to truly take responsibility for living truthfully and in alignment with all that we truly know ourselves to be and to be capable of, as conscious creators of our own individual reality and our collective, Divine, human destiny. To remain in ignorance of these greater aspects of ourselves means that we get looked after and comforted by a host of temporarily satisfying illusions without having to face the journey towards a seemingly more frightening truth in which we are not only the players but also the writers, directors and observers of our own screenplay in the magnificent movie of our lives.

What if we did realise that we could learn kung-fu in 5 minutes; bend reality by simply understanding that "there is no spoon"; begin to see, expose and finally understand all of the external forces which appear to fire endless bullets of undermining, negative paradigms at our poor defenseless "bodies" for what they truly are; and instead of wearing ourselves out with our constant efforts to dodge them, suddenly understood in a single revelatory moment of self-empowerment, that we, pretty soon "won't have to". What if we did suddenly realise, in a single moment, that we are indeed, all-powerful ...what then!?

What then, indeed, my friends, because this is the joyous future we face, and it is now up to us to begin to dream a new, collective, conscious dream of precisely "what then". Blessings and truly enlightened peace to all...

A Message of Love & Hope for Light Workers Everywhere

Hi Everyone,

Season's greetings and abundant love; I hope that this beautiful, bright morning finds you full of the joys of Autumn! Thank you once again for your lovely messages of recognition and warmth; they are both moving and a constant source of further inspiration.

Each week, I ask that what I write should be guided, influenced and inspired by my beautiful writing Guide, Peter. Week after week we have been sending you our messages of hope, love, inspiration, spiritual triumph, ascension and the beautiful vision we are all currently bringing into being with our thoughts our feelings and our constant prayer simply by holding steadfastly to that blessed dream.

This week, my Guide has asked, once again, that I allow him to speak directly through me as he has a very important message for light workers everywhere. This message came rushing through my heart and consciousness as we marvelled at the many Earth Angels and Light workers offering their friendship and guidance to each other through this unlikely technological medium. I feel such gratitude at this time to already be seeing signs that we are, indeed, walking among Angels. Please enjoy this sweet transmission...

I humbly wish now to pay tribute to you, light workers who quietly and mysteriously weave your spell over this troubled earth. Many of you will have an inkling of an idea of a memory of who you are. Some will feel an unexplained affinity with the stars, others will find that you have recently developed a peculiar obsession with Angels and others may feel as though you have suddenly been born anew in a single moment and become a fiery and purposeful individual, who prioritises their spiritual searching, discovery and practice to such an extent that their family no longer even recognises them.

Earth Angels, Walk-ins, Star seeds, enlightened visitors and evolved earth inhabitants, it does not matter so much who you are, for in time, this will once again be revealed to you, from within the enlightenment of your newly opened eyes, within an instant, and has it not been said that we are all sleeping Angels, simply waiting for a Divine call into awakening. What matters most, in the here and now, is what you now choose to do WITH what you are. That glorious being, inter-dimensional traveller, reality-bending-shape-shifter, guardian of the earth and sky, world-mover, cloud-buster, visionary; you have an awesome and untouchable force and an indomitable strength right there in your hands as an awakened being with powerful intent, a human body and mind and that awesome will.

You are a mighty, mighty magician, made from love and walking in light with all of the
necessary dispensation to work miracles from your position of free will upon this wonderful planet of cause and effect. Awaken

now and stir yourself to your pre-ordained responsibilities and go out and fulfil that greater destiny which calls to you even now. Know that you are loved, supported and guided in this, always and in each moment, and that as you step into your truth, the fear, does, indeed, begin to disappear. See how it falls away like an old, worn-out skin. You no longer have need of this, for this is not who you are, dearest one.

Do what is in your heart to perform; what you know is right. Go forward now in full faith because you are what you think you are and what you believe you are here for, is indeed what you came here to do. Shine your light and create waves of love which will undoubtedly wash over all you meet and cleanse them in heart, mind, body, soul and spirit just by the very nature of your presence and proximity.

Call upon all Angels and beings of the highest guidance and the most loving light whenever you see suffering in the world or find yourself in those heavy moments of doubt, and we will be there in an instant. Do not stand and watch and allow yourself to be drawn into guilt, fear or morbid questioning. Begin to overestimate the power of the light you bring to every situation and know that you are exactly where you need to be in every moment and that nothing is by chance.

Become a beacon of light, hope and love, a lighthouse within a raging sea, leading those lost ones into the light, where they too will know, understand and begin to find their way home.

And so it is.

Love and blessings to all...

Living from the Truth of the Heart

In this time of awakening to the truth and spiritual shifting upon our planet, many of us are at times troubled by the question of how to approach the natural changes in friendships and relationships which sometimes come about as a result of our own spiritual growth.

There are many factors which need to be taken into consideration before we can truly evaluate a loving and gentle way to move with these changes, accept them and fully and bless those we love with our truth.

1 We all have a path to walk and the company of those who do not fully love, understand, accept and grow with us is not necessarily helpful or pleasing.

2 If the person or people in question (those about whom you have these worries) were in front of me now instead of you, I would say exactly the same thing to them. In other words, we do not serve anyone by hanging on, 'regardless,' so to speak...

3 We are all, naturally, creatures of joy and Divine beings of great love, capable of great loving. If we are being dishonest with ourselves, or with another, we feel it, they feel it, and this untruth lowers our vibration and deprives the world and the blessed quantum field of our powerful all-moving, change-bringing, soul-stirring, wave-making joy, lightness and love. As we know, friends, our global and our personal evolution walk hand in hand like the very best of friends and the very truest of loves.

4 If you gently and lovingly let go of someone you love but feel you may have outgrown, or a friend whose very presence you have come to dread, they will inevitably find themselves and their own authentic joy much more easily without the hindrance of your apparent perfectionism and tacit disapproval.

5 We are all one and therefore every subtle shift and leaning towards change and truth in 'one,' of us affects the heart mind, soul and being of every 'other'. When you are not being honest about your feelings or friendships, this is usually already known and understood by the person or people involved. They feel it, know it, wrestle with it within themselves and at some level, they may even resent it. Therefore, another wave of unhelpful feeling radiates out into the blessed all and all, creating more confusion, quantum chaos, fear and frustration.

We all face these uncomfortable changes from time to time and those moments of recognition of what we will suddenly no longer tolerate, can be shocking, painful and might at times invoke within us a kind of spiritual stubbornness.

Those of us who have elected to initiate ourselves into early awakening, in this time of approaching ascension, have taken on a loving task of service and, as such, will find that what is being asked of us is at times intense and unreasonably trying, yet the more we try to hold on to the old, the more excruciating these growing pains can seem. It is at times like these that we need to remember that the truth of who we are is love, joy, surrender and connection to The One, and that only that which blinds us from this truth will be removed from our lives.

As we become more sensitive and in tune with our truth, we often find that some of our previously bearable encounters become suddenly and unexpectedly tortuous, even on a physical level and that we are daily, no, almost constantly, being asked to rise to YET ANOTHER new level of truthful living. The cosmos never seems to want to leave us alone. Just when we get comfy again, it opens our eyes just a little bit wider and allows us to see some other new truth we were almost happy to just leave alone there in the darkness.

No one can tell us how to live our lives or what is truly right for us. They don't need to. The answer is already there in our hearts long before we are ready to admit it to ourselves. When we allow ourselves to become truly free, we find it easier to remain joyful and to, therefore, be constantly adding our vibrant presence to the growing song of unmitigated hope and expectation surging across the planet at this current time of soul-shifting transformation. If we limit ourselves, our hearts, our joy or our truth, we limit all possibility which exists across all time and space within which we experience consciousness, both the seen and the unseen; that which is understood and the great unknowable.

Ultimately, when we refuse to close a doorway that leads to more pain, suffering and sadness, we allow it to wander into our lives uninvited at any unguarded moment and suck away our good feeling with a sneer and a whisper.

This is not the time for covering up what we truly feel, however scary the outcome of our disclosures might at first seem. This is simply not what the times require of us; it is quite the opposite. There is no need for us to pretend to be happy when we are not. It is simply our Divine duty to realise that we can create true joy, abundance and happiness simply by saying that it must be so and that life was simply meant to be lived this way.

We have a duty and an obligation to seek out bliss and lightness wherever we can and to spread it wherever we go so that we affect others with our joy and therefore add far more vigour to the ever-patient and loving time line along which we create our most fearless utopia, dearest friends.

We need to ask our selves in each moment, "if I were to believe that my joyful presence and my remaining in lightness and joy in the here and now was enough to make a difference in the awesome cosmic shift currently taking place on our planet, how *could* I become the most joyous, light-filled sparkling being I can be right now?
Would I spend more time with others or more time alone?
Would I treat myself to more lovely things as and when the whim takes me?

Would I dispense with my TV, radio and stop reading those depressing newspapers?

Would I spend more time in meditation, embracing that 'Divine Sweetness'?

Might I spend less time with people who drain me and, if I feel unable to let them go completely, still continue to love them dearly, but see them less?

Would I prioritise fun over work or would I make sure I created work that was so much fun, that there was no difference?

Who would I have to speak to right now about that thing that isn't true for me or for us anymore?

Would I sleep more, sleep less, eat better, eat more, eat less, dance, sing take up the piano, even though I'm now eighty-five years old and can barely move my fingers...bring it!!!

Would I finally, find a way to forgive, let go of the past, grow up, learn to say no, so that those karmic bonds and ties which now seem so suffocating are instantly transformed by the light of your truth and become the blessing that they were truly meant to be? Everything is possible!!

Our suffering serves no one and in lying to another we are only lying to ourselves. The world is waiting for your sparkle, and the Universe is expecting that, as a being created in love and joy, you must have unadulterated bliss, love and lightness for at least a large portion of every day, whatever that truly means to you.

Therefore, be loving, be kind, yet do not cling to the past. Know that all are held within the loving wings of Blessed Angels and the great heart of the blessed all and all. There is none who is higher or lower than yourself, there is simply and a time, a season and a reason for everything and 'this too shall pass'. Therefore do not judge; isn't it quite possible that you might let go of someone, now, because the truth of your heart demands it for your growth, yet find them once again in the afterlife and realise that they are, in fact, a Buddha? Perhaps one who lovingly agreed to create this journey with you for a certain time, in order to lead you onto the shining path...

Therefore friends, begin letting go with love and with kindness towards yourself and each other, live from the truth of the heart, behave in loving ways and allow the truth of true, unconditional love to continually shine into your life and bring you back home to yourself and ever forward on your journey... Wishing you all a Divinely Guided and inspired week and weekend!

Love is the Path

I asked my guides this week what I could write about that would be of some comfort and assistance to those who read these simple posts and blogs on my various networking pages, and they immediately responded with "Write about the path". With this suggestion, they also simultaneously showed me three images. Perhaps they think I'm a bit like Vista! One was the image of Dorothy, whose journey long the yellow brick road leads her to finding the Wizard of Oz and realising that he is in fact not this huge and all-powerful spectre but a small and scared creature who is also in need of courage. They also show me an image of the Red Sea parting for Moses when he tells the Israelites to step forward in faith. Finally, just for good measure, they show me the mists of Avalon which, legend has it, (if my memory serves me well) would only part for those who truly believed in its existence, to reveal a beautiful, mystical and magical place.

My mind immediately took all of this to mean that we should hold onto our faith in the power of our dreams and step forward trusting all the time that the mists will indeed part for us, revealing all that we ever dared to dream of, if we are bold and daring enough to venture forth. At the same time, my heart seems to be calling my attention to the fact that this rush of symbols is also a deeper indication of our need to step boldly onto our spiritual path and remain awake to the possibility that, that which we see around us as fearful and prohibitive is in fact just a reflection of our own distortion of the truth about who we truly are. So what of this distortion? What *is* the spiritual path?

What is the most spiritual way to approach the fulfilling of our dreams and the path upon which we walk as "a spirit-being having a human experience"? Well, to reiterate the overriding point here, love is the true experience of yourself as you truly are, and everything else is, indeed, a distortion and you are an awesome carrier of the love vibration and therefore, as such, will soon see through all illusion of obstacles along your path.

In truth, the path is already *in* the heart and this is why it sometimes bends when we choose with our heads, that which is not in alignment with our highest truth, however, the path never breaks or ends, and we will always somehow be inevitably be brought back to truth, through all of the myriad wonderful and sometimes puzzling experiences we encounter along the way.

There are many ways to achieve our dreams, and yet, why is it that our path is seldom straight, or things sometimes don't work out exactly as we had envisioned them? Lack of faith, loss of courage, failing self-esteem and a belief that we do not truly deserve the riches we sometimes dream of having, embracing and becoming? Yes, prosperity is a natural desire and a wonderful life-affirming freedom, and yes it can be ours when we resonate with it from our hearts, so embrace it! Even you light-workers with your desire to serve and to be pure of intention and of unquestionable integrity, do you not deserve the same freedom and mobility as those who travel across the earth quickly and easily spreading mayhem? Think of all the love you will spread when you are enriched with freedom from worry about how to pay the bills and the joy of knowing that those you love are cared for.

We have the capability within us to achieve anything we set out to achieve, when it is in alignment with love. It isn't something we need to go chasing after; we simply need to allow it. When we truly begin to know ourselves as love, we have all we need. In truth, we are already far richer than we know ourselves to be, because each and every one of us has a Guardian Angel who knows what our heart and spirit most truly desires for our overall evolution and understands our path to true loving service in this lifetime, which is, after all, whether we know it or not, (and whether or not we choose to embrace it in this particular life-span) the true path and the journey for which our hearts truly yearn.

Therefore, simply be who you are in this very moment and embrace all that this means and know, also, that you are still not this; you are something far greater, and to become this being once again is surely, your true loving destiny. Call every day to the highest within yourself and know that the highest within you is love. So that when you wonder about what to do next, how to find yourself, who you are and what you are here on this planet to do, you will simply know that to do the most loving thing you could possibly do right now is surely, "The Path". Then with loving comes more loving and through this exponential outpouring and influx of love you will become the being you are intending to be and find that even though the path sometimes bends, it is simply bending to the tune of that which calls you to once again know yourself as love.

Any practical advice I could now offer in terms of finding the right path, being in the right place, being of the greatest service now seems redundant in the face of this unconditional vibration because it means that to simply trust that we are guided in every minute and to embrace love to the best of our current ability is all we really need to do. As a pragmatist, I have certain issues with that.

What about the right career, the right, actual *vehicle* for this service, this love? What can I tell people about *that*, that will make a difference? What about some of the more practical stuff from my book? (Find Your Purpose, Know Your Path)
The reply is simply this; (to probably paraphrase slightly)

The path *is* love and when what we are living in is truly the vibration of constant loving intention, there is no need to be concerned about "choosing the right path"...it will appear from out of your loving willingness to be guided and to allow it into your life. There is no need to worry about whether you are "in the right place": the right place is always simply in the heart regardless of the geography you recreate in your external world, and in choosing anything from a position of pure unconditional love, how is it possible to do anything *but* make "the right choice"?

Love and blessings to all from the mighty, mighty love which surrounds you even now from within and from all around about you.

Channelling is a Walk in the Park

Many people who would make wonderful channels are often concerned with various factors which they fear might interfere with their veracity and effectiveness. A question many people still ask is

"How do I know it's not just me...how do I know it isn't just my imagination? My guide laughs playfully at this point, as he is often reminding me that imagination, dreams and reality are NOT the separate realities we perceive them to be. "Imagination is simply the doorway to another world; another place in consciousness which is every bit as real as the ground upon which you currently perceive yourself to be placed, only, perhaps, a little more so."

Therefore, however, let us continue to illustrate a point with another one of his beautiful, timely and handy analogies: (By the way, I often find that another sign of channelled guidance, is the sudden 'appearance' of pictures, symbols, metaphors and analogies, which pop into the mind in an instant as a barely formed notion but which carry and entire multi-layered meaning and story within them).

"Imagine that you are walking through a beautiful country landscape in the bright, summer sunshine, noticing things of great beauty all around you. The grass is so green and well cared for, the sky is a wonderful shade of blue you're not even quite sure you've ever seen before. All around you, there are flowers and butterflies exuding a kaleidoscope of colour and richness, which makes you gasp with wonder. As you enjoy your walk and continue to wander through this verdant, technicolour paradise, you become aware that there is someone walking behind you.

It's a subtle feeling at first yet, in time you become affected by this wondrous presence and the effect it seems to be having upon your consciousness. It seems that the beauty of everything you see around you is now somehow amplified by this mysterious companion as you walk. Your steps are lighter and it's almost as if you are being carried along by an injection of love, warmth, understanding, energy and insight, which seem to come from this being.

You are so curious about these new feelings that you turn to see whether there is, in fact, someone there and to find out more about this strange and magical influence which seems to be enhancing your enjoyment to such a degree. As you turn, you notice that the stranger has begun to run to catch up with you, and quite naturally and without thinking or processing the event further, you begin the most sublime conversation which brings laughter, tears of joy and recognition and a feeling that all is right with the world.

In time you realise that your new-found friend is going in another direction and so you bid them good day and continue on you way, still marvelling at the array of rich experience available to you on this precious journey.

After a while, your thoughts turn to your friend once again and as you chance to wonder about them, you suddenly realise that they are, once again, by your side and you are filled with joy, knowing that you will be walking the same road together for quite some time and that, in fact, you do know this person very well. It's just that until you began the walk and raised your awareness fully into the level of, true and natural consciousness and awareness of sublime beauty; you were unable to perceive them.

Now, the walk is whatever you do that brings you joy, writing, singing, dancing, painting drawing, speaking fluently on subjects which please you...

Your appreciation of beauty is your surrender to the flow of true creativity for its own sake.

It is the state of consciousness which allows you to perceive the presence of those who wish to guide you, heal you, attend to matters pertaining to your evolution in this lifetime and, indeed, if you so wish, to speak to and through you for the benefit of all sentient beings including your sweet self.

Your ability to remain open and in this state of appreciation regardless of what feelings, impression, voices, noises, conscious thoughts of being in or out of flow, abandoned by the spirit world or wrapped in Angelic wings might come and go during your creative process... is your ability to become a clear channel.

So during your walk, you were entirely surrendered to the creative process, but you were not clinging to, hoping against hope for, entreating, pleading for or even expecting this or any other form of Divine intervention. When it came, you simply and naturally allowed its magical presence to fill your senses and to enhance your gift of appreciation. At no time on your walk did you stop and ask yourself: *Why can't someone come along who will enhance my enjoyment of this walk?*

When you felt that evolved presence, you didn't ask: '*Now, is this being real and is their contribution to this walk real, or are they and it a mere figment of my imagination? Am I reeeeeeally being influenced by this stranger or is it all just me? Am I really enjoying this walk as much as I think I am or am I just kidding myself?* You continued to walk and everything you desired flowed to you naturally through the same channel of living, loving and allowing within that moment.

When your friend left you, you did not say *Awwww, now it's just me again, it's definitely just boring old me again on some silly old walk.* You knew somehow that you, the walk, the sunshine and the stranger are, indeed, all one thing and all a part of the same beautiful and blessed expressions of joy and love as the trees, the grass and even the carefully crafted shoes on your feet.

When your friend returned and you began to realise that they would perhaps be with you for a lot longer than you had at first thought possible, you didn't huff and sigh or exclaim; *Great, so you finally made it back, good, now the real walk begins again!* You did not cling helplessly to your new friend and say to them: *You are the source of all of the goodness and beauty on this walk; it was nothing until you came along.* You simply allowed for the natural joining and parting rhythm, knowing that there is really no separation between any one being or thing and another and understanding fully that you had only to think of your friend and to quietly request, at any point, that they join you again and they would hear you, however softly you spoke and be with you again in a heartbeat.

Therefore, do what you love to do, for its own lovely sake and ask simply and clearly from the heart, to become a channel for Divine, loving guidance. Endeavour to keep your life simple so that there are spaces in which you can perceive this beauty and magic and hear the voice of God speak to your through its many instruments of beauty and Divinity, make time for a daily practice of meditation or for simply being aware and surrendered fully to the process of Divine creativity and it will come to you naturally and without strain.

Do not question whether it is you or him or her or them. Simply allow it to be and to become what it is and, in time, that which it truly is in nature and in origin will reveal itself to you through your remaining truly open to being a pure channel.

Remember that this is, after all, what it means to be a channel; you must remain completely open so that what you are open to channelling can flow through you easily and naturally. If you are not open, then you are simply blocking the flow, caught up with the ego and its attachments and control mechanisms, and true inspiration never was created thus."

When I first began to write, I had no idea that my writing was being guided. I just thought that I was placed within the creative flow and tuning into some kind of collective, unconscious generic love-vibe or something. I was often moved to tears as I wrote but it was a very long time before I was aware of any particular, specific presence or being, speaking to or through me. I thought that what I was doing was inspired, yes, but in a very generalised way.

Most writers, particularly of 'fiction,' will often say that they feel as though they are channelling the characters they create, yet, bizarrely, still wouldn't attribute this to any particularly paranormal phenomenon.

I wrote because I was literally consumed by a creative flood of pictures, symbols, images, thoughts, feelings, meanings, ideas and intentions, which went absolutely harmoniously hand in hand with everything I thought I already, sort of, understood and believed on a conscious level. What was channelled about that? However, later on, I would find myself frequently crying during the writing of a particular phrase because its sheer beauty seemed beyond description and beyond anything I truly felt I was capable of writing.

These tears were the only outlet for this creative and joyful overwhelm. At other times, I would 'hear' another word suggested to replace the one that had naturally, originally occurred in my own mind and would write it down and question it later. I then began to realise that there were times when I didn't even consciously know the meaning of a word that was being offered, so I would reach for my old friend, the dictionary, only half curious about where this other (better) idea was even coming from. Only to find that not only was the word a much more perfect expression of what I was trying to say but that its particular placing within a few uniquely grouped words did more than just express a sentiment or convey a meaning, they seemed to almost go beyond language and to transfer *into* my being, as I read, a meaning that was visceral and deeply moving on every level.

Another true Angelic trademark – Angelic consciousness seeks to express itself through the medium of transferred experience or conveyed feeling-understanding.
This is the best way I can describe it just now. In time, I began to realise that despite my earlier sense of knowing or understanding certain spiritual truths, I was actually learning as I wrote. My 'aha' moments were no longer the expression of a feeling that; *aha, yes, that would be a great thing to write* but something more like, *aha, so that's how that works then...*

Later on, I began to sense a presence standing behind me, looking over my shoulder as I wrote and offering further suggestions when my own choice of words or phrasing were just a tiny bit short of 'his' idea of perfected sense. The rest of the time I was just in the general inspirational flow.

Eventually, despite my reluctance, I asked in my mind, "Who are you?"

"I'm Peter," he said. "I'm helping you with your writing."

"Oh, okay," I thought, and even though I was struck by the gentleness of this being, the simplicity of the communication, and the feeling that ran through my heart when he spoke almost bringing me to tears, once again, I just said thank you and determined to put him and the whole idea of a separate consciousness, away before the next writing session.

(You might have gathered by now that although I have always been fascinated by channelling, there was some slight resistance on my part). I loved writing, but why, oh why should I now have to go around admitting to people that I was writing all this stuff with the help of a disincarnate being?!!

The next day I had neatly decided that Peter was absolutely a figment of my imagination and everything could go back to being all normal and kind of JK Rowlingish again.

I was humming happily as I began to write the copy for my, then, future website, typing away at something innocuous about, Tales from the Voice of the Heart. I was just in the middle of writing:

I have always been a hopeless romantic and, perhaps, I thought, a little too idealistic when it comes to love. But these stories were touched, also, by some other, mysterious hand which guided mine back from doubt, into weaving around myself these simple stories of love's ineffable and inevitable truth....

Just as I was writing the words, ***"mysterious hand"***, I heard a small voice say "I told you....I'm Peter." It was heart-breaking...at the time anyway. However, to cut a long story fairly short, this was the beginning or rather, the reawakening of a long and beautiful friendship and collaboration and a passionate meeting of 'minds'.

With Angelic Love and Light
Diane & Peter

Courage and Stillness

This week, my guide inspired me to write a short meditation. It seems that there are many people who almost fear meditation because they know that when they allow themselves to become still, even for a few minutes, what they will find in that precious stillness is who they truly are... They know that when they suddenly see themselves, naked, as it were, without that habitual, superficial covering of what they wish to convince themselves is the truth, they might be forced to make changes as a result of this dawning awareness of what is truly, true. How exciting!!!

It is a journey to be greatly anticipated and savoured; that slow unravelling and yet it is indeed only for the courageous of heart and soul. The spiritual warrior who is willing to stand for who they really are regardless of what this might mean. So before we offer this lovely piece, we would like to ask you a question: Which do you believe yourself to be: one who is prepared to go through the fire and the clearing in order to reveal the wellspring of shining beauty, joy and peace within, or one who will be forever tiptoeing around and through the daisies in order to find yet another way of avoiding yourself?

Here's a conversation I had with my guide about my own meditation practice just after writing this week's piece.
Peter: You could perhaps meditate more often now dearest one

Me: But I already meditate every day (hoping he wouldn't draw my attention to the days I

sometimes miss) ...sometimes even twice a day!! If I meditate more frequently, I'll have to meditate 3 times a day!! When will I ever get a life?!!

Peter : It isn't necessary for you to meditate more frequently, just more often...

Me: Hold on a minute but don't those two words mean exactly the same thing?

Peter: Not quite. From where I stand, if I were to ask you to meditate more frequently, you would instantly have in mind a timetable which needs to be set rigidly in stone and filled in with various appointments for things you feel you *must* do, including meditation. There is strain and resistance, and also - I say this with great love - a little childish rebellion. If, on the other hand, I say to you that it would be much to your benefit if at several points during the day, when the need arises, you would draw your attention inwards and towards that greater perspective; that more expanded awareness; that re-connection with Divinity of which you speak, it would be all to the good.

WE both smile.

Please accept the following piece in that same loving spirit from our hearts and from the heart of all things....

Courage and Stillness

Before you speak forget what you were about to say

Forget what you think and remember what you are

Remember that there is nothing else to say

Before you run remember that there is nowhere you need to go

Sip your drink and surrender to the moment

Before you leave remember that your journey has already begun

Before you sleep remember that you are closer to awakening

than you ever were before

Before you wash remember that there is nothing on you that

needs to be cleansed or cleared away

For you are perfect in this moment

Stay a while and remember yourself

Before you hurry remember that there is nothing that will not wait...

you are eternal...

Before you leap remember...

...that you have already begun to fly

The Dance of Love

In these accelerated times, many of us wonder about the constantly changing nature of our relationships. Disheartened with 'failed' relationships yet no longer willing to compromise, many of us seem to be currently wondering where we will ever find someone who can be with us fully throughout the duration of our journey of spiritual awakening and personal evolution, and yet, to some extent, such conjecture only serves to demonstrate that we miss the point entirely. We are (all) 'the journey'.

The dance, the joy, the fun, the learning and the interplay between separateness and unified completion IS the journey and love IS the path. We are all travelling ultimately towards the same blessed destination and in that sense; there is no one who is either above or below us. We only do ourselves a disservice when we see perfection and self-realisation as the urgent goal and not the gentle aspiration. Like our precious, ever-changing hearts, the goal is not a finite thing and every dance within these hearts only brings us ever closer to truly knowing ourselves.

The desire to connect deeply with another being is a natural, human impulse; a soulful longing which stems from our Divine recollection that we are connected to every living being and every spirit essence which ever sprung forth from within the Divine ALL. Yet we sometimes deny ourselves because we understand that we must be complete in ourselves before we will be 'ready' to let someone else love us. Recognising our own completeness, though, means simply understanding that we have a choice in each moment to embrace all that it means to be truly at peace with ourselves. This represents no great mystery and no further challenge because however much we resist it, peace is always calling from within, to be noticed, embraced and lovingly followed in faithful acceptance.

In trusting the wisdom of our hearts and affirming that love is the only truth, we find, within, all of the love the universe has to offer and in letting go of our fears and reaching out to another with an open heart we begin to learn, perhaps through trial and error, that unconditional love is, indeed, the way to true peace.

When we step into an encounter with another person, we must remember always that they are the precious dance of life itself. Because without them, for all the glorious music in the universe, there would be less movement, less creativity and discovery and fewer opportunities to know, to embrace and to truly engage in a dance with ourselves and with the spark of God within us.

When we step out onto the dance floor to engage in a new dance, we allow the heart to simply speak through the body as we become entranced by the magic in the music, the mystery in the movement, and as we move, we find ourselves soundly placed within the seat of our own co-creativity, wonder, surprise and Godliness. Without question, we allow our creativity and movement to remind us to surrender constantly to the beauty, fluidity, discipline and simple complexity of what we truly are.

How much easier it must be to love more fully when we learn how to surrender to love as if it were a playful, expressive dance and to love ourselves and each other with creativity, breathless daring and unrehearsed enchantment...and how much more wonderful and surprising would each encounter be if every time we reach out to touch another human being, we remember that we are about to begin a dance with God.

Mystical, Magical Signs and Wonders

Many of us only ever ask for help from our guides and Guardian Angels when we are in trouble, depressed, unwell, bereaved or so confused that we simply have nowhere else to turn. Of course, they are always guiding us, regardless of our diffidence, gently pointing out the way to peace and hinting at the small steps we might take in order to walk it fully and easily.

When we trust our intuition and begin to wisely follow these small steps, we never know exactly where they might lead. But we must learn to surrender to each new moment of revelation as if it were the most natural thing in the world to do.

Of course, being human, we often struggle against, or question that which feels most natural and right, after all how could life be that simple? How dare I be that happy! How could it possibly be okay for me to suddenly leave my job/start a business/confess undying love to that wonderful person/go back to college/end my marriage or up sticks and start a new life in another country simply because that feels so good, so right and so absolutely Divinely guided? How do we really KNOOOOOWWWW it's the right thing to do? Well for one thing, we are here to DISCOVER how to know a thing is the right thing to do and one way to do that is to DO things; lots and lots of things and observe how they feel. Then, in time, through a process of trial and error and multi-layered experience and observation, we will begin to discern from our emotions, our responses and the subtle energies and laws which govern the universe, the path which will bring us the greatest peace, purpose, joy, fulfilment and personal growth and which, at the same time, allows us to be of the greatest service.

Looking back on our lives, we are seldom filled with regret over the things we did, only those we refused to do when our courage failed us.

I had a wonderful time this weekend at the Mind Body Spirit Festival in Cyprus but it was much more than just a wonderful time; it was a huge, friendly, exciting universal nudge. Last year I spent four months in Cyprus, working on four books, one of which is still in the very final stages of completion. It was such an intensely creative and inspired time that I began to understand, without a doubt, that a large part of the reason I am here on the earth is to teach, inspire, uplift and offer healing and comfort through my writing. When I first returned to the UK at the beginning of the year it was predominantly for family reasons and for as long as I was here, I told myself that it would all work out okay because I was doing the right thing by those I love. Yet, just recently, I struggled with the unhappiness, apathy and low energy that seemed to descend on me particularly in the winter when the grey madness of London's highly controlled, bewildered, automated energy seems to be somehow amplified by its even greyer skies.

Before I went on this trip, I was slightly nervous, knowing that an opportunity to once again experience the joy, freedom and purpose which I associated with being on this wonderful, Mediterranean island might confirm for me, once and for all, the dawning awareness that I would inevitably just HAVE to return. On some level, I didn't want to hear what the universe was showing me because of the huge emotional ties involved. I didn't want to leave my family and friends again and I must say I was finding it hard to trust "the universe".

One particular morning, just as I stepped out of my front door with that thought hanging in the air around me, a large, white feather drifted down towards me, so closely that I simply had to hold out my hand and allow it to fall gently onto it. For days after that, I was literally followed by seagulls; everywhere I went, they were hovering, gliding, soaring and doing strange floaty things above my head. Then there was the white dove in Brixton Market on the day that I asked God, the Universe, Divine Mother, Source, to give me a sign about where I should be living. For some reason this gentle bird seemed such a peculiar sight in the middle of all that concrete, noise and jangly greyness. Surely it belonged somewhere more peaceful, beautiful and natural....Surely all God's creatures do... ?

Eventually, it was time for that short trip away to teach, give readings, catch up with friends and prepare for a date with my old, long-lost love...the ocean. During those blissful few days away, I was absolutely certain of a greater calling to the sacred

Land of Aphrodite and on returning to London after this wonderful, soul-restoring trip, I could literally feel the change in energy frequency as we touched down at Gatwick.

As I stood in line to show my passport on re-entry into what felt almost like another dimension, it was as if I was queuing up to voluntarily climb back into a cage. I noticed all of this and simply allowed myself to make a few observations about what the universe, my body and emotions and the resonant quantum field, with its perfectly, obediently imprinted energies, were all trying to tell me.

This morning, having fallen off the wagon slightly regarding my 'freshly-squeezed-orange-juice-before-anything-else' and become embroiled in a reckless tea and cake regime, I was just pondering what to reach for first, when the top half of my juicer just 'FELL' from the washing-up rack into my uncertain path as I wondered sleepily back from the bathroom.

I laughed and thanked my Guides for reminding me that they are always with me, then vaguely remembered something about having asked, the night before, for some help regarding returning to healthy habits and routines.

We are never alone! We are constantly watched over, loved and guided. We only have to ask for help and we will, indeed, receive it. We just so often forget to ask, or fear that when the answer comes, it will be one we are not so keen to hear, yet throughout even our most challenging times those who silently watch and wait for a word from us can only intercede on our behalf when we ask them to do so.

Sometimes in our lives, we have an inner impulse we just HAVE to follow, regardless of how unrealistic or unreasonable it might seem to us or to those around us. Sometimes when we ignore that call, the pain becomes stronger until we finally begin to surrender to the silent truth within our hearts. We do not always have to know the common sense reason why we have a powerful, intuitive impulse; the uncommon sense of it is always far more exciting anyway.

Neither is it necessary for us to learn only through pain. We can resolve, instead, to teach ourselves how to follow the path to joy without question or restraint. Following the path to joy brings more light to us; light which we are then able to share with others and to add to the vibrant energetic field for the benefit of all sentient beings. There are enough unhappy beings on this planet who have forgotten the simple truth that every creature alive deserves to be happy and at peace. Peace is natural, love is what we are and wonderful things happen when awaken to our truest desires and courageously begin to add our energy and conviction to THIS truth.

So just for today, and tomorrow and for as long as we can remember, let us be brave and daring enough to ask this question of the highest source of Divine Guidance which we feel able to honour within our hearts,

"What is for my highest good and for the highest good of all concerned at this moment?"

and when the answer comes, do not reject it; welcome it into your heart. Smile and say "thank you"...then surrender to its wisdom and follow the path you were born to rediscover in this life- time. Then as you begin to make a habit of asking, surrendering and following, the universe will reward you with peace, stillness and mysterious, magical signs and wonders beyond your wildest imaginings...

Twin Flames and Other Peas

This has been a week of wonderful revelations and learning, as always, yet what feels most important for me to share at this moment, is a little more insight on this beloved journey of soul-mates and the elusive twin flame idyll.

So what about twin flames then? Why is everyone so concerned about them, suddenly? What is so special about the Twin Flame relationship? How can you recognise your own twin when you meet and why on earth does it matter anyway? Well, here are just a few sprinkles of light which we now feel guided to shed regarding the nature of the Twin Flame connection.

Twin flames often reunite during final incarnations in order to facilitate each other's awakening in the final stages of their human evolution, in order to return together to an ascended consciousness. This is why, at this incredible time of global, mass-awakening and ascension, there is such a deep yearning, within so many, to find that other part of the collective consciousness with which he or she belongs or, rather, is most perfectly attuned.

Because you are, in nature, small fragments of that divine spark which holds together the entire being of all things, joining with your twin flame or reconnecting with members of your soul family signifies a willingness to return to that which you were in the very beginning when you first sprung forth from within the heart and mind of the source of all things.

Because your twin and members of your soul group are closer to you in vibration than other beings, they will awaken within you a memory of yourself at a more expanded soul level. There will be a sense of telepathy and of shifting energies when you are in contact with your twin for prolonged periods as both of your light-bodies (or higher aspects of consciousness) vibrate with recognition and seek to bring the rest of the consciousness into alignment with their desired reconnection.

There might also be present, a general sense that they know you far better than they are consciously allowing themselves to admit. You will, in fact, both feel as if you know each other deeply and completely love and accept each other as you are...you barely see yourselves as a separated consciousness and therefore all is understood on every level, all at once, even that which remains unspoken.

All of this is simply the recognition, on the part of your soul, of its close kin or counterpart. It does not, however, indicate that you have found a missing piece of yourself. You are complete as you are. In that sense, although there IS only one thing, one being and one essence from which we all emerge, time and time again, the idea of actually BECOMING 'one' with your twin flame for the rest of eternity, is no more relevant than the idea of becoming 'one' with any other human being, as this would entirely defeat the object and the purpose of this subjective, human experience and the illusion of separateness: which is to learn, to experience, to expand infinitely and to understand a little more about our capacity for loving.

However, finding your twin is admittedly, not like finding any other soul mate. There might, indeed, be many soul-mates: others who have elected to walk a particular path with you in this lifetime. Friends, lovers, siblings, and offspring, or even work colleagues who have chosen to learn a particular lesson with you, teach you some new thing, or meet with you in this lifetime in order to perform a particular service to humanity. Most of these will have shared other lives with you and will, therefore, feel familiar and comfortable to you.

When you meet your twin, however, you will feel a strong and dynamic pull to be together. There will be an electrical quality to your encounters, a deep empathy and a feeling of recognition or of coming home, a feeling that you speak the same language. Most of all, as a result of the dramatic leaps in consciousness usually necessary for twin flames to become harmonised with each other, a typical meeting between them will include the mysterious quality of "setting each other off" in any way which is necessary for both to reach this much desired state of harmony. They will, even unconsciously, serve as a catalyst for change within each other. This change will always bring each one closer to recognising who they truly are and assist them both in understanding and fulfilling their purpose in this lifetime.

If, when you meet this person, they are too deeply wounded to be able to fully love you, you will become a catalyst for their greatest healing. If they are already otherwise occupied in relationship with another, this might cause some pain at the level of the emotions but there will also be an automatic understanding at the level of the soul, that this is what they have chosen and that it will do no party any good for you to wish it otherwise.

Love between twin flames is unconditional, as each soul recognises easily within the other, the unity and the eternal nature of all things and all beings. This is why twin flame meetings offer such a rare opportunity for becoming more loving and for such deep, spiritual understanding and awakening. Some of the conditions twin flames have had to endure at times, require that one or both of them must become almost saintly and this is sometimes, absolutely the point... :-)

Yet, friends, all of this is just a small part of the wondrous truth, and there are many truths which exist between and beyond these shared here now. For, as we know, the journey of us all is to leave no stone unturned in our search for new experience and possibility. We are all assigned to help each other in the raising of our collective vibration at this glorious time of transition and transformation.

Therefore, do not limit yourselves; continue to seek to be all that you can become in this bountiful lifetime and in this tremendous age of awakening, and there will be many more surprises along the way: of that much, you can, indeed, be assured.

If it is to be so, if you are truly ready, you will be with your twin and you will know it. You will come together in service and magnify your love across the earth for the joy and the benefit of all sentient beings. Yet, are there not many peas in this glorious pod, dearest ones? Are there not many hands to hold and hearts to heal?

See the journey of twin flames as the journey of all beings because, in truth, there is only one soul family: that which temporarily springs forth from God in its many forms of expression, in order to truly know itself as love ... and somewhere within the recognition of each part of this wondrous, loving whole, as simply one beautiful thing... is where true peace is found and where the truest of loves lives...

Namaste dearest ALL...

A Journey into the Heart of Love

*'And endlessly throughout this incarnational dance, through
Summers, Autumns Winters and Springs they had both kept this
dream alive in their hearts; the dream that they would one day be
joined, each with the other. And so, faithfully, without having
conscious knowledge of each-other's existence, without each
having even looked upon the other's face, throughout their un-
extraordinary lives they both carried that fire within their hearts
which must one day,* **surely** *bring them together.*

*And even though both were now heart-sick, soul-weary
and tired from the effort of pretending otherwise; of the roles
they played for others, the masks they wore, the masquerade of
false optimism which they played out for the sake of those who
loved them, those who needed them and those who needed for
them to be happy, at night they would dream of each-other and in
the morning they each would forget, and awaken with
unexplained tears on their cheeks.....*

*But the memory was imprinted upon their hearts and even
now when all that kept their bodies alive was the dutiful
inhalation and exhalation of oxygen and the necessary intake of
water and food; it was that forgotten dream, which fuelled the
fires that made their souls agree to go on burning.*

*He knew she would be beautiful when he found her, and
not just because he would simply* **choose** *to love someone*

*beautiful and then trick himself into believing it was her, not this time. He would know her instantly, and because of what her spirit contained, he knew that she **must** be beautiful, for that which is on the inside is often shown on the outside. Her eyes would tell him all he needed to know. Dark eyes; eyes which spoke of many lives lived before, and of suffering endured and then transformed into beauty. They would be deep and wise and wide like oceans and stars and moons. And just as she had turned all of her poisons into medicine, so, too, would all that she touched be transformed, including him. She would bring him back to life and teach him the secrets of the heart and he would share with her; his strength, his devotion and the wisdom of the ages.*

And she knew that he would sparkle like the golden sun because they both carried within them that same light, and it was rich and warm and glistened like sand and made others want to be near to it.

*Sometimes others would fight possessively among themselves for her time and attention or try to restrict her movements so that they could stay close to her light a little longer and warm their spirits with remembrances of that which she now embodied and which her soul was destined never to forget. Sometimes it drained her and made her almost weary of living. Perhaps it was the same with him. Or perhaps they also gathered around **him** like moths around a flame and he would lovingly show them the way back to their **own** light. Such a man she could love deeply. But such a man would be desired by others also...*

*She would be careful and keep the contents of her heart safe. She
would leave him clues and speak to him in his dreams and in
codes which his heart alone could understand.*

*One day, she quite unexpectedly walked into a room that
(without her knowing) the Angels had compelled her to enter. It
was a day like any other. A day when she felt more or less as she
had felt the day before - for this was an all too regular
occurrence - except that this day held **him** within its hours and,
so, in this way, it was to be a day **unlike** any other she had ever
known. Soon he was there up close to her just as she had known
all along he one day would be and with one look between them,
one heart, one mind, the same wide awake look, the same fire in
his heart and his eyes as in hers, the same longing...to belong...
to someone, the right someone... everything that there was to
know about their past, their present, their future and the path that
they would walk together, was known to them in an instant. And
all that ever was and ever would be between them was wrapped
up in that moment, when she reached out and felt his hand;
warm, strong and full of certainty, reaching out to shake hers,
like a long lost friend.*

*His eyes followed her and when they looked at each-
other, all at once the essence between them conspired itself into a
sparkling radiance so that they would both know what they had
found. And now it was no longer a matter of 'if' but of 'when'.
For both knew that however long it took, however many obstacles
they would have to overcome and however many doubts, fears,*

oceans, mountains or any other geographies or dramas cared to intrude upon their destiny, their certain joining was now the one beautiful, brave inevitability in a vast sea of probabilities.

When they finally came together, they were still young enough to enjoy each-other and yet not so young as to waste a second of the time which would now undoubtedly run through the days all too quickly. And when they kissed for the first time, it was as if the Universe held its breath for a moment and then shuddered with the sheer delight of its plan's fulfilment.'

"And don't tell me...*they lived happily ever after.*" A surly-faced man sitting at the back of the encampment muttered cynically as he leant forward and glared at the old story-teller. He was rewarded with appreciative guffaws and giggles from the assembled crowd. The story-teller could see that he was waiting for a response. None came. Instead she turned and looked at him sagely, but still she said nothing. "Why do you fill our heads with these dreams when you know that they are not real? Such things are not possible. Such meetings happen only in fairy tales. We are not children...we do not want your dreams, we do not *need* your stories."

The storyteller looked sad for a moment, and then smiled gently at the man.

"Everything begins with a dream." She said. "Or have you forgotten? Your life was once a dream in the mind of God. Do you not remember how your life began? Or his smiling face as he blew you gently, lovingly from his hand like a kiss into the world and into your mere *dream* of an existence?" The man laughed loudly and sneered nastily.

"First of all, she tells me stories meant for children and *now* she thinks I can remember what happened to me when I was a baby ...or before I was even born!!!" He screamed with laughter now, enthralled by his own wit. "And how can you say that life is a dream? Don't you think I know what is real and what is a dream? And who are you to speak of such things as God? Who knows what God does or what he thinks? Who knows even if God *himself* is real?" There was a less laughter now as the man's anger at the world ripped through the air. And slowly those who were either too embarrassed to stay or too thirsty for the dream's sweet nectar to linger a while longer in their hearts like fine wine on the palette, quietly began to take their leave. Some mumbled their goodnights, while others shuffled off quietly to their tents leaving the surly man and the story-teller to end the night together...

"And how do *you* know what is real?" asked the story-teller, undaunted.

"Ridiculous question, I know that something is real because I seeeee it," the man elongated the word for emphasis then continued with his spiteful tirade. "I can *touch* it." He said touching his robe. "*This....* is real,' He held up a piece of the material for her inspection. 'I can see it, I can feel it....it's real."

"Hmmm..." The story-teller was bemused. "So *if you can feel it, it is real*...interesting." She paused for a moment as if she was learning from what he had told her, and then she continued. "And how do you *feel* something?"

The man replied breathlessly, without even thinking...what was there to think about?

"Why, with my hand of course. If I feel this saddle, it has substance and form, it feels warm to the touch...it is very real, is it not?"

"Ah yes, I'm sure it is just as you say, but you cannot touch or feel the thoughts in your head, for example, can you? So that must mean that *they* are not real."

The man seemed unseated for a second then quickly regained his composure.

"Ah now you are trying to trick me! You want me to say that my thoughts are not real so that you can say that I, too, am a crazy person like you; a dreamer, a weaver of tales, a crafter of fantastical trinkets with which you decorate the feckless minds of these fragile innocents you gather around you each night."

The woman smiled. This took him a little by surprise because it was a smile so full of love that the man felt something strange stirring within him. This was not right! He wanted an argument!! He was just beginning to get into his stride and now, here was this woman this... riddler, (probably she was a reader of fortunes, also, for all he knew) trying to melt away his antagonistic zeal with some bewildering affectation. All the same, he *was* moved.

"Ah ha, you felt something didn't you, but not with your hand, it was with your heart that you knew it." The old woman was triumphant. She closed in on him, now warming to her subject. "But was it ...real, I wonder, let me see now. Is *this* real?" She lifted up her hand and held it against his cheek for just a second. And as she did so, she looked deeply into his eyes and, smiling once again in that strange and loving way, which had irritated him so, seemed to penetrate his soul with unfamiliar and somewhat frightening warmth. Until, all at once, he felt himself, as he knew himself to be, slowly unravelling. In an instant, he found himself weeping and sighing helplessly and uncontrollably, gasping for fitful breaths, as if breathing his very own life into his body for the first time, or maybe even some new life-form, so strange was the sensation.

"What did you do to me?" He gasped.

"I simply introduced you to yourself and to the magnificent beauty of your own ever-loving heart." The story teller fell silent and waited as the man purged himself of pain that seemed to be centuries old and several lifetimes in hurting. When the sobbing began to subside, the story-teller looked into the man's face and saw that he was changed a little, for the better. Some of the harshness was gone and she now looked upon the face of The God Within him.

"Why were you crying?" she asked in a way that suggested she already knew the answer.

"I don't know," he sniffed. "I felt something strange, which came upon me suddenly, something which moved deep within me. I can't explain it, like my heart was so full of love, I felt it fit for bursting... and so I had to let some of this love, this overflowing feeling, erupt out through my tears, and yet all of this took place within an instant, and was so deeply strange and mysterious and took place without my proper prior consideration. I, I..." The man was babbling incoherently now. He stared at the ground, puzzled and a little shamed by his own outburst. "I don't understand what happened." He confessed, now slightly humbled.

"It did really happen then?" Again the story-teller already knew the answer to her question. Why was she goading him like this? "So it *was* real and not, for example, a dream?"

"No...I...I..no. Yes, it *was* real. I know it was real."

"So you are willing to accept, then, that something happened to you just now that you couldn't see or touch or even understand, but it was real to you even though you don't *know,* exactly, what it was?"

"Yes, yes...." he cried allowing some of his confusion to escape, his unanswered questions hanging in the air, unformed and unspoken.

"So how do you *know* it was real?"

"I JUST *KNOW,"* he said.

The man stared out into the night, his head swimming with alcohol and challenge, his voice, when it came, an impassioned whisper.

"...because I *felt* it." Nothing moved as the man stared at the ground and tried to absorb what he himself had just said.

The woman laughed. She knew that there was a good chance that in the morning, all of this would be forgotten or that the man, if he did remember, would question himself in the cold light of day, until he was eventually able to laugh off the experience as one of those wild imaginings which sometimes followed a particularly rich ingestion of wine, late at night, when all is shadows and strange matters... and noises. Even now, so soon after the experience, he was already turning it over in his mind asking himself whether this might all be just a dream.

"We are always dreaming" she said. "We are all, all of us, always dreaming... and all things begin, as but a dream."
She was now beginning to unnerve him. Had she really just read his thoughts so readily and without effort or strain? What if she was from some other world, come to steal his soul away? He had heard of stories like that, strange things happening out in the wilds in the dead of night when no one else was around to see what transpired and the one poor creature involved never lived to tell the tale. But then he wasn't sure he believed in having a soul, as such. Life was too hard to believe in such things. You hope for something better and you end up with just your dreams and nothing to show. Do dreams put food in your mouth or buy you a

decent bed to rest on at night? Why did he have to go and open his big mouth? Why hadn't he just kept quiet like everyone else? Surely there was no way back from a happening like this...to the land of the living.

He was startled out of his reverie once again as she threw a white cloak over her head and beckoned him to follow her. "Wake up unbeliever, you were lost in a dream of your own making....*wake-up*" she whispered, "and we will weave wonders in your life and out in the world, and you will shine your light forth for all who come after to follow."

'Such strange words,' he thought to himself, *'why do they make me shudder so?'*

He followed the woman as he somehow knew he must. Was she doing this to him? Did she have him under some strange spell perhaps? Although he questioned it briefly, it was with that same, hitherto estranged, '*knowing*' that he came to understand that, in truth, these were *his* feet which now stepped one in front of the other to follow her and it was *his* heart that somehow bade him to go. Down a long path and into a winding labyrinth with so many twists and turns that he began to feel dizzy. He knew, nonetheless, that there was something waiting up ahead for him which would change him forever.

"Where are you taking me?"

"To a place where you can find that which you seek"

"But I am seeking nothing," he said.

"And yet your heart cried out to me..." she muttered into the night. "There it is again. Can you hear it?"

Can you hear it? Can you hear it? The wind echoed.

Can you hear it? The trees whispered.

"Can you hear it?" She repeated. "Can you hear the voice of your heart?" And then she was gone.

He found himself in a small clearing at the centre of a very deep maze, with no apparent means of escape. He panicked.

"Story-teller...where are you? Come back here now!!!"

"Here now, here now, can you hear it? Can you hear it?" All that was heard was the mocking of the wind as it ran angrily through the trees, and the sound of his cries and his own sobbing, echoing back to him through the night. It was dark, he was alone and there were all kinds of creatures which might beset him in the darkness. Why had he followed her? Why was he here at all when he could have been tucked up under a blanket pleasantly drunk and secretly dreaming of lost love, just as he did every night when no one was there to read his face and call him a hapless dreamer?

He wasn't going to let them think he was like all those other fools at camp; hanging on to her every word as though their lives depended on a happy outcome to some unlikely yarn. Night after night he'd scoffed at her stories under his breath, and swelled with false pride as the others enjoyed his engaging repartee at the story-teller's expense. His own little side-show every night which served a dual purpose, he thought, of winning him popularity and also showing how strong and courageous he was and what a good leader he would one day make. And yet, once alone with himself in the loneliest hours at the end of every day, enveloped inside all of the all-encompassing emptiness of each night, in truth, it was the old woman's stories that kept him alive with hope.

And long after all others were fast asleep, her voice and her words would ceaselessly taunt him until sleep, at last, mercifully arrived to lead him, kindly, into a few short hours of silent respite. If he could just prove her wrong, or get her to *admit* that she was wrong, about hope, about love, about this dream of *happily ever after*, he could maybe stop the hurting which came from too much hoping... for that which one cannot have.

And yet he prayed every night as tears fell around his noble face... "Oh God, please send me someone to love....before my heart withers away and dies, right here in this very bed, and forces my body to give up on life, some cold and callous night when nothing moves within me anymore, not even my own blood." Now, even the old crone had left him. Why was he so unlucky with women?

"Old Woman...!!!" he shouted angrily. "You come back HERE NOW!!!!" He cried and shook all through the night. He thought he heard laughter. His mother's voice rang around the labyrinth and then the voice of every woman he had ever known and everything he had ever said to each one came back to haunt him, their faces looming up over him until, as in some strange mirror, he saw himself as each one. And as he did so, each one would disappear as fast as it had come and another would appear. All night this continued until he found that he could no longer wrestle with himself, for it *was* he alone who sat in the clearing. And in his recognition of *himself* in each of these apparitions which he sought to chastise, he suddenly saw the futility of his struggle. And so he quietly and lovingly let each one go, one by one until only a single voice remained.

In the morning, he was still alone. Trapped *and* alone, his two worst fears combined. With all the voices now gone, all was eerily still and sombrely quiet. He wondered what would happen next. Somewhere off in the distance, he thought he heard voices from the encampment, although he couldn't be entirely sure that he was still living in the same world as the one which they inhabited. But he felt calm. Some new feeling was beginning to grow inside him and he had no choice but to just let go and give in to it. He realized now that he might well die in this place, and somehow he made peace with it.

"My life is as nothing now anyway," he reasoned silently. "Let me starve to death or be eaten by wolves or devoured by the night itself, and then maybe my remains will be found lying here, by one who *truly* loves me and it will be just like in the old woman's stories. Then at least my life will have meant something, my dreams will not have been for nothing. I will be loved at last and at the same time, freed by death...yes, loved *and* free."

On the third day, the story-teller re-appeared.

"Ah, you're still here" She announced rather irritatingly.

"Where else would I be?" The man asked petulantly. His face was drawn and he seemed exhausted. He was hungry and cold and his dry tongue gripped the roof of his mouth and made his voice sound strange, but he was no longer angry with her, or, for some reason, entirely surprised to see her again.

"I thought you might have found your way out," she said, giving him a large drink of water from a copper tankard. He gripped the tankard as if it might disappear without a firm enough grasp. It felt very real, very real indeed. He gulped deeply at the water's cool cleanness while never once taking his eyes away from her face. She looked different, today ...younger, fresher, more kind somehow...He smiled despite himself.

"Who are you?" He asked reaching out to touch her without spilling a drop of the precious liquid. She leapt away from him, looking startled for the first time ever, since he'd known her.

"Do not touch me," she said... "For I am not what you understand me to be."

She sat down beside him on the dewy grass, but her robe was unchanged by the wetness on the ground and unsullied by the grass-stains which now covered his clothes.

"Why didn't you leave this place?" She asked him matter-of-factly, as if it were the easiest thing in
the world for him to have done.

"What do you mean? How *could* I leave? This is the most fearsome labyrinth I have ever seen! I knew I'd get lost if I tried to find my way out of it. So I just waited. I knew also that you'd come back if I waited long enough. I can see that you are a good woman."

"Hah! You know a lot of things ...don't you?" She said. "You knew that you wouldn't find your way out and you were right, because you didn't even try! You just sat here all this time weeping and moaning and waiting for me to come and save you, when you could have just got up and walked and found yourself on the other side..."
He knew that she was right and that something new was happening to him again, just as it always did whenever he saw her.

"Why are you being so cruel?" He asked.

"Why don't you try *knowing* that you *will* find your way?" She smiled with deep affection and before disappearing once again.

"WHAT?!!" The man began to laugh to himself, out loud, standing there alone in the clearing looking like a man who had lost all reason. It was no longer his usual embittered laugh though, but a sound which was strange to his ears. It was the sound of a happy man, happily laughing at himself..... How could it be that he was standing half-starved in this green wilderness after days, no, maybe years, no... perhaps a *lifetime* of confusion and fear, laughing with real, deep and meaningful joy? He felt strangely liberated. Her words floated back to him through the labyrinth.

"You know a lot of things ...don't you?" "Why don't you try **knowing** *that you will find your way?"*

"I will know then" he said to himself. **"I DO KNOW...... because I will now *choose* to know. I know the way, I know it now,"** he announced excitedly to the labyrinth. **"I know the way, and now I will walk it."**

He spoke, but it wasn't his own voice speaking, at least, not his usual voice.

"And I can show you how if you let me." A gentle smile rippled through his heart as *it* suddenly understood that he was now listening to it, at last, probably for the first time and perhaps even for the last, but for a moment, at least, and for now, that was just enough. He stood up and began to walk.

"*This way,*" it seemed to say.

"And now, I will know that my heart is right," he told himself. "For that is what I am now choosing to know."

"Now go that way," It said, and he followed where it led.

"Speak heart," he cried joyously, "I hear you now. Speak louder."

"Listen" came the reply. **"I am here now. I am speaking to you always. I have spoken to you since the very beginning. I am**

still speaking now. And as you listen, I will grow louder." He continued like this a short while and in a few moments, the mystery of that painful labyrinth which had earlier seemed to represent hours, days even, of potential trial and difficulty, was now unravelled and revealed before his incredulous eyes in an instant! Outside the labyrinth, the beautiful story-teller stood waiting.

"What kept you?" she said, her laughing eyes shining from her, now, even younger face. The wonderful man he had become, laughed and laughed and laughed... at her, at himself, at the world and its beautiful simplicity, hiding behind a complex series of excuses for *not knowing*, not *letting go and allowing the heart to speak* its singular truth about love and about the journey one should take to find it.

"None come to love but through the heart." She stated simply. It was so obvious now, why had he not seen it?

"Then it's no wonder I have been so alone." He said. "My heart was a locked door where none could enter and nothing passed through. And all the time I cried out vainly for love and thought I knew love, yet failed to see the truth of it right here in front of my eyes." Now all at once, he truly loved every small and every large thing upon the Earth and felt compassion for, and a need to share his heart with, every person and every living thing that had taught him to love this way and helped him to find out the truth about love. And all at once he knew that *all is love* and that all else is a lie, an illusion, perhaps even a bad dream from which we must all wake up. He forgave himself for all his past mistakes and forgave all those who had wronged him. He even felt a deep and irrational love for the story-teller, now and wondered why he couldn't touch her, hold her even, and maybe one day ... kiss her, love her, find out whether she was a real woman or just a figment of his fertile imagination.

Yet he didn't trouble himself when she was gone once more because he was so full of
love and full of *knowing* that she *was* real and that he *would* see her again. His heart knew it, for she had taught him the secrets of the heart and he would always listen to the truth of it, and the truth was that she was now a part of him forever.

The sun was shining as he walked back to the camp, a changed man. No one noticed him as he walked past, as all were involved in some kind of mourning. Suddenly it dawned upon him that it was *he* whom they were mourning and he felt pained to see how much love he had failed to notice in all the time that he had travelled and lived among them as the fearful and closed-up man he'd been before. Yet even as that wretched creature so full of rage and scorn, who cried alone at night, he was loved.

Of course no one recognised him now, this man who had journeyed into the very heart of love, died and been reborn. And so, for a while, he walked among his old friends as a stranger until in time they came to accept him as one of their own, this new, happy traveller who had happened into their lives with a warm and infectious smile and an open heart.

They gave him a special place to sleep at night, near to the important elders of the clan, and everyone said that he would make a handsome and just leader one day because of his kindness and the great love which shone from his adorable face.

One day, he was coming back from gathering wood for the fire when he saw a beautiful woman, sitting on a log. She wore a white robe, which was damp and stained from where she had been sitting on the dewy grass earlier that day. His heart leapt for he knew her at once.

"What kept you?" he asked, expecting her to laugh again in that playful way and to perhaps now tease him about his earlier arrogance or his time spent in the clearing at the centre of the labyrinth where he had heard his heart speak for the first time, made peace with himself and become a man who was now truly free to love. But instead, she seemed confused; it was as if she didn't know ...and so he chose to let the subject go.

She offered him a tankard of water and they chatted away like old friends, well into the sunset and through to the next morning, the smiles never once leaving their faces. He stared in wonder as he gradually took in all of who she was. And her face hurt from smiling with the sheer joy of simply being with him this way. And so it went with them for quite some time, loving, laughing, dancing eyes and meaningful smiles, whose meanings only they two understood, hearts ablaze and as hungry and thirsty for each-other's words, minds, bodies and the joining of their souls as ever two people were.

He never spoke of the story-teller or of his time in the labyrinth. He had long ago decided that some things are better left unsaid.....so that we can perhaps hear them more clearly.

But sometimes, he would have a strange dream about a man who feared the night and despised his own bed; A man who wished to be devoured by hungry wolves rather than to feed the ravenous wailings of his own heart. A man who believed that he could never find love and that dreams were like fool's gold, sparkling meaninglessly to lure you into the rocks. And he would awaken smiling as the sun rose each morning, relieved and grateful that he could now breathe life into a new dream of his choosing...

And as for the story-teller...well, she learnt that even though everything does *indeed* begin with a dream, there *is* a time and a season for everything under the sun; a time for stories and a time to live...a time for dreams and a time for waking. For even though the dreamer is nothing without the dream, what good is the dream without the dreamer? And they lived happily ever after.

A Christmas Message

With the approach of the Christmas season, many of us will be excited, making preparations and enjoying all of the seasonal magic that comes with this wonderful time of year. The songs, the lights, the smell of cinnamon, the late-opening shops, the very thought of the lovely presents we'll buy for those we love and their happy little faces when they open them up on Christmas morning.

People of many different religions, creeds and belief systems who do not even subscribe to the ideas woven around this specific day will, nevertheless, be affected by its ebullient energies. I tend to get quite giddy at Christmas from the excitement and the profusion of goodwill energy that's suddenly floating around. Many of us, though, will not be so willingly enthused by this collective joie de vivre and will, instead, be dreading the Christmas season.

Perhaps you are feeling depressed and alone. Perhaps you are about to lose someone you love dearly. Perhaps you are concerned about financial difficulties and won't be able to give your children the kind of Christmas you usually do. Perhaps you have nothing and are sleeping rough. Or perhaps this year has not proven to be what you'd hoped it would be and you'll be quite glad to see the end of it. Perhaps you think you have no one to love or you are newly divorced and adjusting to taking care of your children alone and trying to make things work for everyone. Or there might be a chance that your only concern is that you have not fulfilled all of the goals and ambitions you set for yourself at the beginning of the year.

Perhaps you are the misunderstood person in your family, the baddie, the one who is the repository for all of the unconscious "stuff" they don't want to look at. Perhaps you are the one who does all of the growth work while all they appear to do is blame you for standing in your the truth and light and insisting that they reach up for higher ground if they wish to meet you. Perhaps you are standing right now on hallowed ground, if only you did but know it. Perhaps you know you have some tough decisions to make in order to create true happiness in your life next year. Well, I cannot claim to have the answers to all of these challenges, but I have faced most of them at some point in my life and here are a few tips I'd like to offer to anyone who is uncertain about the joy and wonder which is available to us all at this magical time.

If you are afraid of being depressed and alone on Christmas day, remember that you were depressed and alone yesterday and the day before and ask yourself what difference it will make feeling that way on Christmas day. When you get to that magical part of the day when you really feel sorry for yourself, use a pen, a journal, the power of the brainstorm and the magic of Christmas to intend that life will never, ever find you this way again on ANY other day and to decide how and why you are going to create something better next year. Enjoy the silence, enjoy the stillness, enjoy having time to yourself to start hatching a better plan, dreaming a brighter dream and creating it by writing a few pertinent steps in your 2009 diary that will lead you towards fulfilling it...

Or pick up the phone. SOMEONE out there is probably longing to hear from you!!! If you can think of absolutely no one who wants to hear from you, call upon your Angels; they will guide you to a happier truth...

If you are in conflict with someone and can find no peace in your heart, sit down for 5 minutes, close your eyes and ask your Guardian Angels to show you a way to find peace and to bring peace into the hearts of all concerned. Christmas is the perfect time for miracles; expect one!

If you are about to lose someone close to you, let go with love. Christmas is such an incredible time of year with all of those wonderful positive, energies lighting up the heavens far more than we can even begin to understand just yet. If someone you love is leaving the earth at this time, know that they have chosen this time because with so much love and goodwill filling up the radiant field, they know that as soon as they let go, they will be carried along on its joyful stream and be sure to easily find their way to the place of their choosing. They will feel your love more strongly than ever at the moment you let go and they will always, always be with you. Give them the gift of letting go and living a fuller live now than you have ever lived before, in their honour. Notice that the only thing that they are taking with them is the love. Give more of it, by setting them free.

If you are concerned about money, focus on the little things. See this as an opportunity to teach your children about love. Buy less but give more: more hugs more smiles, more "well done"s more "thank you, I love you"s. Get into the kitchen and start baking together. Think of ten games you can play which require only pens, paper and wit. Let go of the pressure to buy anyone anything that requests batteries or uses up more precious electricity. Create a list of ways that this Christmas is going to be more exciting than ever because you have less money blocking your imagination. Let it flow, let it grow and watch everything your heart truly desires come bounding into your life, over the next year, like a friendly puppy, encouraged by your playful, gentle attitude of surrender.

If you have even one person to hold and to love at some point over the Christmas period, you have wealth beyond measure. If even one person says 'I love you' and truly means it, you have found true gold. Buy tiny presents but give them with great love and you will learn much more about loving and see how much you are truly loved for who you are. Your wealth is not determined by what you own but by what you feel able to give. Set new criteria for what true wealth is. Get excited about the simple riches you already have...and share them extravagantly...

If you have tough decisions to make about next year, allow that process to invigorate you rather than scare you. Allow the coming changes to make you feel even more alive!!! It's wonderful that there are still changes and growth in your life. Enjoy simplifying, re-inventing, downsizing or upgrading alike. Greet them all with the same enthusiasm, because whatever you have, whatever you lose, whatever or whoever you perceive yourself to be in this moment, what you are really doing is dreaming a new dream for how your life can be and allowing the light of a new consciousness to enfold you, to reveal you and to lead you closer to truth. If this year has not been all that you hoped it might be, remember to notice how far you've come and think of all the wonderful things you can bring to the world next year.

If your own family cannot bear to be with you and have cast you out because you remind them too much of the pains of the past and all else that they do not wish to see, remember that you are simply showing them the truth. A true spiritual warrior answers only to the truth and follows only the love and the light. Trust that part of yourself which bravely carries the wisdom of true love into your family in this lifetime. They might never understand you. They might never see the richness of all that you bring. They might never see you as you are, but some day, someone will and they will thank you for it.

Continue to love and to love and to love even more. Whatever happens, the truth you let into your heart and allow to shine through you, shines out into the world and creates a better world for YOUR children and make no mistake about this. YOUR children will love you immeasurably and understand you deeply. They are the future. Create the future and do not let the past convince you of its power and validity in your life. Plant your seeds and leave them alone to grow. Let nature and the changing seasons grow them for you in the fullness of time. If there is no one to champion you, do not spend a second feeling sorry for yourself. Find someone else who needs a champion. You will be amazed to discover how fortunate you really are and how much love can grow from the love you give. Even the hardest of hearts is only temporarily lost, out looking for love.

If you have absolutely everything to be happy about, make sure that someone in your neighbourhood, about whom you might have a secret, nagging concern, also has something to feel good about. Go out there now, TONIGHT and become someone else's Christmas Angel.

If you are destitute and sleeping rough, hold on...I have just sent an Angel to be by your side...

TO everyone who has come to me for readings, coaching, workshops, books or who has enjoyed reading these simple offerings, thank you thank you thank you for the joy you have brought into my life this breath-taking year. Thank you for the opportunity to express God's love for you and to learn to love more. Next year, I hope to love and serve you again. If you've enjoyed reading these messages, please post this group as a gift for your friends so that they, too, can enjoy a regular burst of uplifting inspiration.

For now, lovely friends, from me; my Guides; your Guides; all of the Blessed Angels who work with us and through us in love and light; from my God and your God and a host of Heavenly Stewards and loved ones ...whoever you are and whatever and however you are
celebrating...
Brightest Season's Greetings and a very Merry Christmas!

A Message for the New Year

This week it's my great pleasure, once again, to allow my guide and Angelic Guardians to
bring another message through my heart into yours. My deepest wish is that the year
ahead is filled with love and happiness for us all, for what else is there in life that truly matters...

As this New Year dawns and we find ourselves in the midst of great change; change which requires of us even greater courage and faith, let us remember, now, that we are stronger than we ever were. We are beginning to awaken, once more, to the light we carry within; strong, warm and certain; rising up from of our darkness and dazzling, like an ever-blazing sun. Let us remember that when we set our intentions upon something, it is there, it exists 'out there' somewhere in the radiant stream waiting to become a reality.

Let us remember that what we now see around us is the result of our focus upon a new time of peace and awakening to all that we truly are. Let us remember, also, that this change, although heralded by a turbulent transition, ultimately shows us the way to true peace and understanding of ourselves, our connection with each other and our responsibility in creating the world of our choosing. Let us also remember that fun and lightness can always be employed to assist us in bringing great change. They uplift us and those we love and add to the light and the potential for ease and fluidity in traversing these seemingly unpredictable times.

Flow into these changes without resistance. Let go, laugh and let love work its quiet magic. Focus on what unifies and brings truth; the simple truth that we are
all one being waiting to be born anew into a time of joy, peace and expanded consciousness of all that is. Let this be a year in which we honour the simple truth of the heart and its quiet wisdom.

The heart knows that the only teaching we truly need is how to follow its promptings, and that in the end, all that we have to give is our love. Yet, even if the only goal we have this year is to become far more loving than we ever were before, the fulfilment of this goal would shape worlds and, yes, move mountains. For even when our faith fluctuates, if we know how to truly love, we have the greatest of all gifts. The awesome power of love is what created us.

Yet, even with the great endowment of free will and all that this playful, rogue
element brings, we are, still, or at least, we appear to be, at worst, perhaps, 80% love and 20% uncertainty and discovery.
Therefore, let us let love be what we discover this year and let our awareness of our choice in all things, become our only certainty.

Be Beautiful Sometimes

Wherever you live...

...live with passion

Wherever you go...

...go with the flow

Whatever you see...

...see it with your heart

Whenever you run..

run with a smile

Whoever you are...

...is just a disguise for your true beauty

Whatever else you do this year...

Love fully...

Live well...

...and be beautiful, sometimes...

The Heart of Purpose

So what is it that stops us doing what we know in our hearts needs to be done; what we know we are here to do? Well sometimes it's fear, sometimes it's uncertainty about the future, sometimes it's simply because we temporarily lose our way and wonder what on earth we were thinking of, having such bold and daring plans. Other times we simply know somewhere deep inside, that we are not trusting what is true for us and are, instead, about to venture into doing what we think we *should* do simply because we can.

As light workers, we know that we each have a Divine purpose to fulfil in this incredible time of shift in global and dimensional consciousness. As assorted sensitive beings, we may have elected to experience certain challenges in life, which we hope will, ultimately, lead us to greater levels of awareness, empathy and learning, about love and the human condition. Yet these very challenges can sometimes create personality traits which, if we do not have the wisdom to see and to transmute them for the higher learning they offer, can make our path seem a little fragile: over-empathising with every passing feeling and sentiment from those around us about what is right for us; an overburdening sense of collective responsibility which leaves us exhausted before we even begin; an unhealthy tendency towards self-sacrifice and concern for others and a careless disregard for our own feelings and intuitions.

So we boldly step into the process of trusting our vision and re-making our lives anew and at first we are so certain of our dreams and our intent, yet in the very precious early stages of creation, we are sometimes easily swayed by other influences which seem to act as untimely tests of our strength, resolve and conviction to truly stand by what we know in our hearts to be true.

As ever-evolving beings on a journey towards fulfilment, purpose and loving service, we are faced constantly with endless possibility and choice and it is our very nature as creative beings which often tempts us into exploring every possibility before finally having the courage to draw a line in the sand and say this is who I am and this is my truth, when in the very next moment we know we will be presented with yet another aspect of self, yet another possible truth and so the search for the truest truth continues.

Yet, there is an infinite, Divine truth which resides somewhere within each one of us: the truth that we are, at heart, infinitely loving beings with the desire to bring the greatest love, joy, peace and enlightenment to the greatest number of the souls with whom we come into contact and whichever is the brightest way that we can do this whilst also bringing the greatest degree of love, joy, peace and enlightenment into our own being might perhaps be the truest truth...

As I sit here and write these words, my heart is radiating warmth and happiness, having such a great passion for the written word and a sometimes overwhelming love and respect for this blessed process and the connection with the very many sources of inspiration which even now seem to gather around me in an ever-patient throng. Also knowing that what I write might touch the hearts of others who resonate with these experiences, moves me to continue sharing these simple insights.

Many of us recognise that we are here to serve, yet this service must, surely, be joyful in order to be true. We were not put on this earth to suffer endlessly. We would not serve food to a friend from a broken bowl, so why would we offer ourselves in service in a way that we find unfulfilling.

Of course, any act of service is a great joy for all, and when we are called upon to step-up in small, unforeseen eventualities, we do so happily, thankful for the opportunity to love. We would not stand on the side-lines and ask; 'Hmmm but if I help this person to cross the road or give up my seat, how much will I enjoy myself? Is it really going to be a treat helping this person to carry their shopping home? **They** seem to be struggling themselves, how much fun am **I** gonna have here?' Our response is quick, natural, human and spontaneous...usually... and seeing the difference that we can make to someone else, even in a small way, lets us know that we have, indeed, served a purpose in that moment. At other times we are simply stirred by a cause or concern and in that very moment of awakening, we act without thought of reward. Yet if what we do to in order to offer ourselves in service on a day-to day basis creates a conflict with what makes us truly happy, then we are surely serving food to a friend from a broken bowl.

We are all perfect creations, fashioned in the image of perfection and when we come to understand, accept and surrender to that Divine perfection within us, we quickly discover that whoever we truly are and whatever we would choose to offer of ourselves happily, abundantly, lovingly and unconditionally is, surely, our most propitious purpose and our most perfect path, because love **is** the path and simply doing what we love allows us to become even more loving as our journey continues to unfold.

Permit such a great love to find you, prove you, move you, change you make waves in you until you eventually succumb to all that is true...for you... Let go of any rigidity in seeking to find yourself, and simply remember who you are. Then, as our slightly annoyed, indigo teenagers might say, ...'allow it'!

Water

Water flows
Stick breaks
Dry stick breaks faster and creates dust
Heart whispers
Mind shouts
Whatever else you think you understand...
...The truth is you
Do not judge it
Listen to it
Trust it
Love it
Hold it gently in your hands
Like a tiny bird
Until it noisily spreads its irrepressible wings
And takes to silent, potent flight
Love waits
You are an unravelling work of perfection
Slowly revealing itself through time, patience, irritation and love
The pearl within the shell
The diamond-in-waiting

All love and gratitude to the Heavenly Beings and Divine,
Angelic Messengers who inspire all earthly treasures...

Yes We Did

We have no idea who we are or what we are truly capable of creating until we begin to embrace an awareness of ourselves as powerful co-creators of our own reality, but true and lasting change comes only when we realise that this is just the beginning. The mind is the great protector, yet the spirit simply knows it is safe, the spirit is eternal and the heart is its sweet messenger.

Even when we are at our most lost or uncertain and feeling our strongest tests of faith, the spirit knows that we are not our minds, bodies, words, actions, behaviours, beliefs or fears. The spirit knows that our limited awareness of who we might be, even at a soul-level consciousness, while we exist within this short time & perceived reality is not who we are in its entirety. The spirit knows that we are not our political systems or the inequities in our society or our world. The spirit knows that all things are possible and that ultimate, infinite change, beyond anything we ever dared to imagine, even in our most utopian dreams, does not depend on any one individual or group of individuals. It is an impulse which suddenly stirs within the collective heart and awakens it to the possibility of finally, truly desiring something better, and this can occur in a second of awakening with just the right catalysts.

We are very fortunate at this time to be surrounded by such catalysts. You, yourself are a catalyst for unprecedented change and simply by believing that you can be, you begin the journey towards personal and universal awakening. Your prayers are heard, your intention is felt, you do, indeed, create change and your purposefulness of spirit is absolutely appreciated. You are a greatly loved & precious light-worker.

I often imagine that in this great shift in global consciousness, we are all playing a wonderful part in bringing about our awakening. Whether we do this predominantly through working on the mind, the body or the spirit, we are all a part of one glorious, awakening collective, integrated continuum through which humanity seeks to heal and to grow itself far beyond what it might otherwise become.

We owe it to ourselves and our children to continue to mould our beautiful new world into being with our consistent thoughts of beauty, trust, love and harmony, until it is done. We must reach out into the very ethers themselves and continue to mould this dream with our own fiery hearts, our loving hands and our wildest imaginings. If we are serious about dreaming our awakening into being and creating a peaceful, loving earth in which the heart, spirit and soul are the only true leaders, we must continue to keep our focus on thoughts of unity and all that truly brings us together ignoring, to the best of our ability, the illusion of separateness. If we fall into that trap, we will have been fooled once again.

I am not a political animal as I truly believe that lasting change will come only as the result of a global shift in consciousness, a change in hearts and minds, of the kind we currently find ourselves experiencing at this point. However, this very important inauguration is, for me, a wonderful, heart-warming affirmation of that very transformation. It provides for us all, an external, physical, beautifully personified symbol of that blessed shift and of all that we are capable of dreaming into being when we are truly ready for another stage of heart, mind and soul evolution.

The American voters chose to embrace this dream by electing an audacious light-worker into the white house and therefore all of humanity, as a connected, vibrant, awakening mass-consciousness, chose it. We selected and attracted it from out of the infinite range of energetic possibilities which lay around about us, within the collective field. As a unified, shifting, evolving consciousness, we chose peace, racial equality, the healing of a wounded past, harmony, integration, love, awakening; eternal, everlasting hope and the optimism of the visionary. Whatever we believe ourselves to believe, whatever we feel truly matters today and whatever happens from this point forward, it is incumbent upon us all to remember that these are the things we chose: Love, life, peace, harmony, healing and hope. **Yes we did...**

Open

Open gate
The wind walks away
And waits

Open door
The doubt shuffles in
Step out

Open mind
A bright light shines through
Let it

Open heart
You are that great light
Stand tall

Valentine, Shmallentine

It's nearly Valentine's day again and many who consider themselves to be either too evolved or intellectual to take it seriously can easily become, respectively, convinced that:
a)it's nonsense to let the calendar tell us when to express love and celebrate its life-affirming, world-changing, healing and transformative qualities and/or
b)it's all just another commercialist plot to divest us of our senses and money, through advertising, guilt and coupley, adult peer-pressure.

If you're single, you will probably not fail to notice that you are suddenly surrounded by ecstatically embroiled couples, heart-shaped balloons, teddy bears, flowers and other peoples' exciting dinner plans. You might also notice that, suddenly, another year has passed when, despite the fact that you decided, almost precisely this time last year, that **next year,** i.e. NOW, you would absolutely have sorted the 'situation' out and be relishing the joys of true, deep and meaningful intimacy and long-term loved-up-ness, you're somehow still alone again in February.

At some point in the year, despite your best intentions, perhaps you were thwarted by your shyness, your true feelings about intimacy and commitment, your apathy, lethargy or obsessive workaholism ...or your fears and limiting beliefs about love and relationships. Or perhaps it was your rebellious insistence, during those blessed moments of sweet, unimpeded solitude, that you absolutely adore your own company too much to ever have to 'put up with' anyone else's for an unspecified (and therefore, possibly endless) volume of time. Their expectations, habits and desire to evaluate, analyse, dissect and wallow in every aspect of one-to-one coupley minutiae. Why would you choose this when there's a world of responsible, self-determined, globally-aware, short-term acquaintances and fellow, evolved beings with whom we can share uncomplicated and inspired connections and be

on our merry way in a matter of minutes, days or weeks? Each of these blessed encounters leaving us with the feeling of having truly touched someone's life, yet not ever challenging us to venture into the depths of our ability to grow with another person or to embrace our soul's deeper longing for something more substantial than the next lovingly and cheerfully offered Goethe quote.

Once again, I am not preaching from some higher plane, friends, I too am in the thick of it! It's all good! It's, surely, very evolved to learn to love and to enjoy spending time with the person who has the biggest influence over the direction and quality of your life...you. It's also very much evolved to be able to relate to someone in that deeper, more intimate sense. It's very evolved to understand that we are **all one** and that every offering of love which brings light to another, even for an instant, ultimately brings light to all and does far more for our evolution than we may, as yet, realise. It's also very evolved NOT to do this, or even be aware of such principles, but to simply be at peace with everything we do.

It's evolved to decide that you're not happy about the way things are in your love-life and to come up with a plan for making changes. There comes a time for action, a time to heal and a time to move on from the past. There also comes a time to be honest about whether you feel truly ready to be in a relationship or whether you're 'just not that into it' at the moment. Then perhaps there's the opportunity to live happily with your current choice instead of pretending to yourself that you long to be with someone while continually self-sabotaging by seeking out a succession of unavailables and fellow commitment- phobics. Even the fear can be healed when we at least begin to acknowledge it. Evolution is love; love is evolution, and love heals all: therefore, love all of your choices. They are all evolved. Living is evolving, loving is evolving, breathing is evolving, the very nature of what it means to be evolving...is evolving, even now. Do not even believe what is written here. When tomorrow comes...it and I will have evolved beyond this truth and be seeking some new concept.

There is also an evolved alternative to **all** of this, and to the usual scurry for personal validation through hastily constructed mass-marketed plastic gifts and generic, seasonal sentiments. It is to simply become aware that there is a wonderful energy which gathers in the ethers whenever we all, en-masse, turn our thoughts towards love: It's an energy that can be utilised by all who wish to embrace it, grow it and send it out to add vigour to that bright possibility in which we become the most universally loving people, society or world we possibly can.

The next time you come across a large, red or pink heart in a florist's window, imagine it growing, glowing and reaching out to cover and encapsulate the entire world. Imagine Angels carrying hearts of all shapes, sizes and colours to parts of the world in which the populations truly have good reason to believe that they are without love and that the rest of the world has abandoned them. Send out thoughts of love to all those who have truly been used or betrayed. Send love to all those who feel truly unable to forgive. Send anonymous flowers to someone who might feel lonely, whether you know them intimately or not and whether or not you have 'designs' on them.

If you're part of a couple, stay in love whatever happens. This can be a testing time!! I've seen many a wonderful pairing fall into confusion and disarray for just one day in the year, as disgruntled partners, with very high expectations, suddenly begin to rely on the day's offerings as a marker of the depth and veracity of the other's love. Forget about it! Detach from the expectation. Be kind to yourself. Communicate with each other, heart to heart and, if necessary, **say** what you'd like. Do something different. Do something beautiful and loving for someone you don't even know, so that whatever happens, you will spread more love and still feel full of love.

If you're single and are able to spend the evening feeling at peace, you will be truly loving yourself. You're not out trawling clubs and bars in drunken desperation. You are stepping off the wheel to enrich and acknowledge yourself and to, perhaps, become more aware of your truer, deeper desires and motivations.

And as for the soulful singles and deeply divining daters, we are the lucky ones this year. We can take our time. The air is positively charged with the energy of transformation and global evolution. This means that the chances of connecting with a true soul mate or twin flame are much amplified by the compelling call to alignment which is carried to us, even now, on the blessed winds of change. We know that something is coming, something big and when it does we will be free and ready to give it our undivided attention. We know how to play and to explore and enjoy this loving feeling in all its aspects. We know that there is a time and a season for everything under the sun.

This is the time to be still and know that love is, indeed, on the way now. We also know that when it does arrive, this one life-changing romance is not the be all and end all, or indeed, even an end unto itself. Love is a journey which has no beginning and no end and our loving nature continues to radiate out into the ALL, long after we have said goodnight or heard "I'll call you." We know that in a sense, this *is* just another day, and just such another opportunity to love.

We have heart, soul, dignity, compounding consciousness of all that we contain. We have magical presence, and the attractive, irresistible drawing power that comes from quiet, yet unbridled courage, endlessly faithful anticipation of good things and a deep, inner knowing that 'groove is in the heart' and that when the lover is truly ready, the *true* beloved will, indeed, appear.

There is nothing to prove and no one to tussle with except yourself so spend the evening celebrating the fact that you still know how to love and that somewhere, someone very precious is waiting for you, looking out for you. Someone very precious who will relish the true, spectacular wonder of you and the magic in you that makes you choose to wait ...for someone very precious.

Namaste, lovers, ALL

Hearts and Feathers

Well, what an interesting year it's proving to be already. So far, for me, it's been a year of going deeper into the heart and developing even clearer communication between dimensions; cleansing and releasing the past and more of those old, worn out energies and situations and having the courage to keep saying yes to a new kind of light and energy frequency. At the moment, I feel very aware of this, ultimately glorious (although sometimes, somewhat gory) process both personally and globally. The duality debate and the waves of 'negotiation' continue to swill around the cosmos, keeping sensitive souls awake at night!...All who have 'ears to hear' will know exactly what I mean. Keep heart. be 'of good courage'

Keep on keeping on. The journey and the destination are both within us because we are the golden city, if we only did but know it. WE are the grail! The lights are shining brightly, many great hearts are aflame and the Angels adore us much more than we can even begin to imagine.

Continue to hold as much light as you possibly can in that flaming heart of yours, just by being happy, optimistic, laughing, dancing, smiling or simply, quietly shining when your energy isn't quite up to the full all-singing all dancing gig. However you might feel right now, like everything else, it's transitory...

The Magic of the Ocean

Sharing things of great beauty with each other increases our feelings of joy, wonder, optimism and evolution towards becoming the kind of beings who CAN live comfortably in a brighter world, a world of love, peace; far less contrasting duality and much magnified light. We all have our moments of doubt, but there are always many ways to rise above them and to once again touch those moments of clarity, grace and true perspective. So this is it; this is just another one of those ways; the beautiful water; the ocean.

You might have 'heard' me waxing on about the wonders of the ocean many times before but actually being this close to it for these few blissful weeks gives me an opportunity to really take in the magic and to contemplate and attempt to describe, for your happiness and mine, the true wonder and the inspired gift that this breath-taking body of water represents.

As I gaze upon the sea, I am transported far away on its glowing, flowing, knowing rhythm and each wave reminds me of the waves of being; the unplanned and unrehearsed dance which is, nevertheless, somehow perfect, beguiling, indescribably satisfying to behold and totally sensible in the most irrational and wonderful way.

As I watch the minuscule drops of twinkling, effervescent spray dancing on the waves, they remind me that there is always potential for the greatest and most surprising magic, held within the tiniest and seemingly most insignificant moment, event or person and each of these can be transformed instantaneously, in the heart, into a magnificent blessing.

As I observe how the sea moves shamelessly, unapologetically, simply being exactly what it is, no more no less, it makes me gasp at the wisdom of its composure. We have a lot to learn from the sea. All at once it is angry, effusive, sparkling, radiant, choppy; a cacophony of madness and seeming disarray and yet, it always knows exactly what it is, why it is and where it is going. Without explanation, it is simply as it was meant to be. Without question, it continues, knowing that it brings something nothing else can bring. It never gazes at the moon or stars, wondering about whether it might be nicer to be one of them. It simply knows, obeys the pull of the moon and the call of the wind and answers only to the temperature of God which moves within it and calls it either to stillness or to wretched, wrathful cleansing, in any given moment.

The sea bathes, heals, nurtures, transmutes, transports and washes away the energetic cares of the unseen world. It is filled with salts and minerals which bring a blessing to the personal energy field and a boost to the physical body. Bursting with Divine energy and essential vigour, it is also calm, serene and gentle.

It doesn't weep, yet it is constantly flowing. Nothing is wasted. Not one drop.

It is one with the moon and stars and knows that there is no separation between them.

Sometimes at night, instead of slipping into a dream, I slip into the sea and remember that I am you and you are me.

This time of year always reminds me of the time of the wonderful and wise prophet, Jesus and his beautiful followers. I now know why they always walked beside the sea. And yes, I know that the Bible has been much adulterated and that many Christian festivals were created from out of the ashes of ancient mythology and the dates are all wrong. But pretty soon, many of us will turn our thoughts towards remembrances of the archetypal, historical moment of great shift in consciousness still represented, for many, by the Easter period and might do well to also remember some of the practices of the many masters who have come before to show us the way to ascension.

They didn't sit for hours in front of computer screens as we do now. They engaged almost constantly with the forces of nature and therefore never questioned their role in its grand scheme.

We are in the midst of great change and it would perhaps serve us well at this time to show our children and to remind ourselves regularly of the power of simply getting out into those places where we can hear the winds of change blowing and feel the very breath of God leaping in our lungs.

The sea rolls along as it does, simply because it must. Do what you must, what is in your nature and allow it, also, to be subject to the changing winds...Because the time is coming when all that we know will be unrecognisable and all that we understand will be changed in an instant.

Being 80% water, we already understand the magic of the sea, the mystery of the saltiness...somewhere deep inside us...we know it. We remember...Breathe it in...

Sleeping Gods

Today I sat and wondered how it would feel to be an atheist, to not have any place in my heart for any concept of a Divine being or aspect whatsoever, even one I called something like "source energy" or "The universe". What would it feel like to just have no feeling whatsoever, of anything indescribably sublime and greater, more powerful than myself but of which I was still an essential part, despite its greatness? How would it feel not to have a sense of being metaphysically connected to every other being on this planet and in this great universe, regardless of what name I chose to give to the spaces between us? It felt a bit like trying to pretend I had never tasted chocolate ice-cream or coconut milk and cacao smoothies or trying to imagine that I'd never ever ran through the ocean with little bubbles of cool foam bursting in refreshingly enthusiastic joy all over my feet. It was like trying to imagine I'd never seen a sunset or a sunflower and didn't know about that sudden, sunny madness that could make you gasp with irrational, awe-struck happiness... It was like trying to imagine I'd never, ever loved anyone or anything ...ever....

How would I explain the beauty of the night sky now? ...Or Van Gough or Mozart? How could I ever listen to Dr. King's *I have a dream* speech and rationalise away those goose-pimples? How could I make sense of Mahalia Jackson's heart-stirring talent or Michael Jackson's *Dangerous* choreography? How could I possibly understand the power and beauty of those exquisitely paranormal and Divine models of self-expression and mastery as purely human or even scientific phenomena? (Newtonian, not quantum physics...which is, after all, constantly hinting at God and Godlike human qualities anyway, albeit through a very cold and theoretical series of baffling, cloak-and dagger-communications. Come right out and say it pepes...we created the universe WITH God and continue to do so and it scares the bejesus out of some of us!!!).

Anyway, the more I thought about it, the more curious I began to feel. In fact, I actually started to feel a bit frustrated. I was being deprived of an experience! What does it FEEL like to be an atheist, I mused, for want of something better to do. What did you pray to? Who wrote your books and blogs for you? And where did all the love go? What would you do with it all?

'I've got an idea,' I said to God, who had been listening intently to my peculiar train of thought, 'I'm going to spend the rest of the day pretending I don't believe in you...just to see how it feels.'

G – Okay, yes, that sounds like fun. I'm going to try it as well. Let's do it! For the rest of the day, I'm going to pretend I don't believe in you...just to see how it feels!

Long pause

Me – Hmmm...now THAT doesn't sound like SUCH a great idea... !!!!!

Long Pause

G – Hmmmmm... I know what you mean...

Long Pause

G - Back to work...?

Me –Yeah, yeah............sure.............. sure...

Well, that's almost it for now friends. I'm trying to stick with my determination to respect your time by keeping these communications short and snappy, even though there's SO much more I want to say!!! Thank you for sharing this moment. I hope that whatever you believe in, whatever your God is, whether or not you choose to have one, you believe in something, anything, beyond this three dimensional awareness of yourself, that can stir your soul into greatness and remind you of your awesome creative power. Most of all, I hope you understand that whatever you choose, you are still a work of perfection, a cellular explosion waiting to ignite, a holy rolling stone, waiting to gather momentum! God doesn't care if you're an atheist. God probably completely respects your choice and admires your refusal to accept a set of doctrines and dilutions on pure here-say. I think God probably gets it!

I wonder who God would prefer to hang out with – an allegedly devout lunatic who uses God's alleged words to create conflict, suffering and personal strife, and uphold an age-old system of human enslavement and self-doubt, or a loving atheist with a great sense of humour and a Centerpoint standing order? It's a feeling thing, a thing that lives miles apart from a far-reaching range of descriptive possibilities, and God probably loves nothing more that a good laugh at our inability to grasp her/his/its true nature. But I'll bet, these days, The source of all creativity and wonderful infinite choice is beginning to marvel at our burgeoning understanding!

For me, the whole God thing is a personal , visceral thing. It's not something you can understand with your brain. It has to be alive in your heart before you can really know it. And once you know it, there's just no way of UN-knowing it again. The idea that it and I are not separate is no longer just a theory. God expressing itself as Diane, who is sitting here at this laptop, for the most part, unaware of a universe of paranormal activity that forms itself around her to create just one treasured, perfect moment of thought and feeling.
Experiment today, with knowing yourself as God as you go about expressing your creative impulses and your loving stirrings... just to see how it feels.

Dear friends, whoever you pray to and whatever your beliefs, I hope that someday soon, an undefined and unconditional quality of rousing and magnificent love will rampage through your heart and awaken you to yourself, as a little fragment of sleeping-God who is capable of shaping beautiful worlds! Do not hang your head in doubt or cower away in the darkness, awaiting a judgement you don't believe in!! Do not analyse your way into another angry, anti-something corner. Lift your head and heart and once again say, with Godlike force and fury...LET THERE BE LIGHT!!
Precious friends, Namaste…I truly honour the Divine in you.

A Lightworker's Prayer

This prayer came to me recently as I basked in the gentle afterglow of that beautiful wave of 10.10.10 energy. I've noticed something very interesting since that day: A huge shift in our consciousness towards a deeper understanding of our truly Divine nature. It's no longer just words. We are beginning to experience ourselves as little pieces of the source of all loving, creative light, this magnificent flame of unquenchable consciousness, expressing itself through these little men and women's bodies and minds. And as I sit here now, after such a long process of cleansing and personal realignment, in what feels like the calm after the energetic storms, I am amazed at the speed and scale of the changes taking place all around us. Thank you for being patient with me. I know my communication over the past year has been a bit "random" as my daughters might say. There are some very mysterious aspects of the ascension process, as you know, and the last year or so has been a pretty intense time for many...

Another thing I have noticed recently is a reprioritisation of what is truly important to us in our lives and a deeper awareness of what is purely illusory. What is it that we really need in order to feel at peace with ourselves and how do we reconcile our previous desires and ambitions with our sudden recognition of the transient nature of the things of the physical plane. Almost overnight, there seems to be a new consciousness emerging and it feels to me, suspiciously like the energy of the fifth dimension!!! Here on earth!!!!We ARE breaking through. Love is breaking through, spectacularly!!!

Please enjoy this prayer, share it freely, credit the author and stay in touch with us.

Love, light and peace

Diane

A Light-worker's Prayer

Great Spirit, Divine loving light, if I can walk with your song in my heart everyday; if you guide my steps constantly; if you speak to me in the stillness, clearly and with strength and I often choose to listen. If I can find a way to love you, to serve you, to heal and uplift those you send to me for this purpose, if my children are fulfilled and happy and walk with you and your Angels constantly. If I always have food and drink from your plants, trees and rain and I can always grow and bless the earth as they do: naturally; according to your will and the laws of nature. If I can soothe the hearts of the world-weary, by allowing you to rush, unhindered, through these walking words, my open heart and these burning hands. If I can stand aside as you reach out to lead them gently back into your care; You who needs no name but has many; You – the Divine, all-knowing, infinitely loving centre of each bright soul. If I always have a safe and comfortable place to sleep at night and sunshine on my face by day, reminding me of your warmth and those gentle, loving rays that bless me constantly through the cold. If I can examine my heart, with kindly eyes and say, with honour that I have loved you with every inch of my being and sought you constantly. If you are suddenly revealed to me again and again in new and enriching ways, touching my every breath with the true miracles that come just from knowing and loving the fiery heart of you... then my life will be well lived and my job well done.

Divine, loving light, teach me to be humble when my ambitions and plans tempt me to stray from your sweetness. Help me to understand that nothing is more precious than your love and I will allow it into my heart whenever I am humble enough to know that I am only human and courageous enough to remember that I am Divine.

Because nothing else is real except the love that flows through this heart from the infinite source of all loving light and creation, yet, even this limitless love needs attention. Like the fruits of the abundant vine, passing through time, it comes to nothing if it is not harvested respectfully and shared abundantly.

Help me to always be mindful of love with a heart-full of love and to remember that love heals all, saves all, cures all, moves all and in the end *is* all... Teach me to surrender all things to a higher and higher love.

And if I can find one thing on this earth so sweet as this love, then I will cling to it as I cling to you. And if just one lover exists who understands and shares my love for you or whose embrace touches me in the deepest parts of my soul, those that only you have ever reached before, then maybe, I will fall in love.

Until then, and happily, ever after, I am swimming in love, bathing in love and truly falling into love. You fill me up and I am a channel, a vessel for the Divine truth of true love.

Great Spirit, Father/Mother/Lover-God, do not let me be shaken by criticism or praise. Let me remember often, to step fully into my true light, away from the deceptions and seductions of the mind. Whatever comes and goes, let me shine steadily in each moment, knowing that only love is infinite and everlasting. Help me to walk my path in full faith, even when I fear my life might look absurd to others. Help me to expect and see the best in others and to be as open to receiving love as I am to giving love. Help me to go within to find what truly matters, to rise above the seemingly disastrous and teach others to do the same, seeing wisdom in everything and resisting the temptation to fall into despair. Or to constantly seek the advice of others, knowing all the while that all great counsel comes from within…from the heart you've made your home, in just an instant.

Help me to trust. Teach me to surrender. Make me kinder, wiser, stronger. Strengthen my faith, love, hope and charity - and, yes, the greatest of these *is* love - and I will share this love, simply with my willingness to let it flow through me, without attachment to where it goes or who it touches because attachment is not love. Love is its own sweet thing, for its own sweet name's sake, flowing through all other things, with a unconditional kiss, like an unrehearsed song.

Bright loving light, expose me when I am hiding away in fear or indulging in false modesty. Great Spirit, move me and show me when to rise up and step up and when to be still and find the heart of my life, letting all else pass away. Let me feel the certainty of the flow of your loving direction, daily. Teach me how to bend with it and stop the struggle I sometimes have with life. Love does not struggle.

Help me to use my co-creative power, to create things of beauty that benefit the ALL. Help me to find the exquisiteness within the depths of my soul that inspires me to create things of great beauty, simply for the joy of creating things of great beauty. Help me to co-create my life with love, from love, FOR love, to create more love and to express love in everything knowing all the time that nothing comes from me, only through me on the crest of that same sacred wave, which IS love.

And if all this is not enough, then you will show me the way to do more and I will try to follow you in full faith. Yet you and I will always belong to each other, one way or another, just as the leaves belong to the tree and even as they fall, they nurture the soil in which it stands. It always was and ever shall be. I am your flowering and your birth. You are my centre, my trunk on this earth. Love is the constant, watering stream.

The living, loving, wandering gleam
Stillness: the rock over which it flows.

And peace is the path and the seed that we sow.

Deep in my heart, Mother, Father, Loving Light, I already know who and what I am. Help me to know it more, to be it now and to live, love and express it ALL for love's sake, shining my light, living my truth and inevitably serving my purpose, whenever I am serving love.

Divine, loving spirit within, wherever we lead me, let there always be hot showers and scented soap, merry souls, good books and occasionally, yes…roses.

Only Love is Real

This week, I'd just like to respond to a debate that was sparked by my first blog in this series, *A Lightworker's Prayer*. Well, okay, it was more a question than a debate. Come to think of it, it was actually more of an *implication* than a question but it was there, nevertheless, just kind of ...hanging in the air between friends and asking something like this... "so....don't you think there's any space within the consciousness of a true lightworker for desiring and enjoying material abundance?"

So the first thing that comes to mind is that, A lightworker's prayer is simply that, *a* lightworker's, *this* lightworker's prayer ...of surrender, non-attachment and the sincere desire to allow love to be the strongest motivation for everything I might achieve in this life and a statement of loving intent and deep, deep gratitude for what already is ...right NOW, rather than a request for poverty. Lol!!! Poverty is deeply unpleasant, although, admittedly, much less so when you're surrounded by fruit trees and sunshine.

Yet, there is surely no greater wealth than knowing what you love and empowering yourself with the ability to get into a feel-good, in love with the world, loving and benevolent space. And that's not always easy when the current system of exchange insists that money is our God and therefore those who have it are saved from a mediocre life, delivered mercifully from their 'quiet desperation' and handed paradise on a series of exotic, hand-painted plates while those who don't, will have to interminably suffer sackcloth, ashes and material hell-fire and damnation. (Just going to extremes to make my point)

However, thankfully, yes, some of the most beautiful, inspired, spiritual souls on the planet are very wealthy and long may this trend continue to spread. I would suspect that during these times of energetic shift and Divine realignment, these souls might have felt an even greater burst of altruism. There are no judgements towards those who aspire to the empowerment that wealth can offer. It's just perhaps important to notice, once again, that only love is real and everything else IS simply demonstrating varying degrees of illusion! However, the need to suffer impoverishment in order to prove one's goodness is also an illusion. In context, it's actually all okay. It's all just whatever it is!! The light of new consciousness is shining irrepressibly through the cracks of our limited, black and white understanding and transforming everything it touches, slowly illuminating all great beauty and all great injustice alike so why worry.

Trust your heart, follow your joy!!! You were put on this earth for your own specific, magical purpose and there are no contradictions in a fifth dimensional space, just love, truthful self-expression, unified consciousness, understanding and the balancing of all things. Everything can exist in harmony. The 5th dimension is simply love and love never makes us wrong! In and of itself, there is nothing wrong with wealth or striving to be wealthy or showing others how to become financially free! In fact, how can it be more correct that greed and corruption are so richly rewarded in our society while those with genuine goodness in their hearts and a deep desire to serve are constantly told that they should do what they do for free, only for the love of it! There are no "should"s in this dimension. All are free to choose but I suspect that if the world's wealth was suddenly in the hands of those who place loving service at the top of their priorities, the world would change over night... Oh, yes, under our current (woefully outworn and primitive) system (of exchanging things of great value for little pieces of metal and paper) in the right hands, money can spread loving feelings like wildfire!!! But the attachment ... Aye, there's the rub!

The desperate worship of anything outside ourselves will only ever serve to impoverish us spiritually and increase the illusions of separation which encourage us to justify our cruelty towards each other. The idea that one thing or being can have supremacy over another and that this falsely elevated position can bring satisfaction in and of itself, is as futile as the idea that if I have "financial security," this will mean anything at all to me when I breathe my last, physical breath.

So as far as wealth goes, enjoy it if you have it. Live the life you love and be who you are at the highest, loving expression of yourself, whatever this means. But don't be fooled into thinking that your wealth makes you 'somebody' or conned into thinking that poverty is a virtue. Become a shining inspiration rather than a dull and soulless aspiration or a sallow and turgid martyr. Burn brightly from INSIDE, without compromise, knowing all the while, that you could walk away at any moment if seeking your true path demanded this.

And this too: Know that you are always abundantly rich whenever your heart is light and your spirit is truly free.

Thank you for raising these inspired questions. Your responses and enquiries are such a blessing!!!

The Power of the Heart

I'm smiling as I begin this blog because it touches a very deep chord within me and I'm sure many of you will also resonate with it. Almost immediately after writing my first blog in this series, I began to get into a slight panic about what on earth I was going to write in the next one. After the Light-worker's Prayer, I just didn't feel as if there was much more I wanted to say but there was a blog now! And a blog had to be filled didn't it? A blog had to be logging SOMETHING, didn't it? Of course, there were things I wanted to write about, tons of things I wanted to share, but there was just no real flow in any of them; they just weren't in my heart. They were all in my head! There was so much I wanted to say about so many hot topics of the day. So much crazy stuff was happening 'out there', surely there was stuff that needed to be said about it all….now!! But somehow, nothing was moving me to open up a new word document, and even when I forced myself to, somehow the fingers just wouldn't move across the keys. Every time I thought of something that seemed important to say, I just froze up inside and somehow couldn't feel the inspired voices in my head that always helped me to find a beautiful way to say what needed to be said. So I asked my guides, "What's going on? Why haven't I 'got' something?"

And the reply I received was something like this…"Why do you need it now? Why is quantity so important to you? Does giving a lot have to mean …producing a lot? What if that one prayer could heal a thousand hearts? What would you choose to write now?" I was stumped! But surely, I needed to have a few things lined up, at least so I'd know there was going to be….something there on a regular basis!!!

"And what if that one prayer, the one which was destined to heal a thousand hearts, was the only thing you ever communicated, what then?" I thought for a minute. Surely the whole point of all of this was to create something that was meaningful and of benefit, so who was I to judge what that might be, how much of it might appear on a page… and when. But it was still baffling. Surely my guides weren't actually saying that there WOULD only ever be one message on this blog!!

Suddenly, the word "attachment" was there again, hovering in the air like a hungry gull, waiting to suck away my usual enthusiasm and the unbridled joy I customarily felt at racing my fingers over the keyboard, imagining I was like Mozart, only with words instead of notes. And now I understand what it all means. So here is a timely, seasonal light-worker message for seasoned light-workers everywhere, and just in time for the Winter Solstice/Christmas period; with all of its potential swings and roundabouts; joys and tears; tantrums and tensions or, perhaps (for those who have been preparing for a utopia for some decades now…) peace, perfect peace…

The quality of who we are and our loving soul's intent to become more loving is surely the greatest gift we can ever give to the world, and it is what we choose to do from THAT consciousness, every day, in every waking moment that marks us out as true beings of love-light consciousness, whether we give that gift through a smile; a kind word; a choice to love instead of react, or the simple gift of being able to truly touch another human being's heart, in just the right moment, in a way that makes them instantly remember that they too are full of loving light…. Yes, there is indeed a time to stand up and be counted, a time to be heard, a time to fight for what is right and to expose the imbalances and injustices taking place all around us.

And there is also a time to remember that we are infinitely more powerful than any of the illusory tricks and traps, which might attempt to knock us off balance and tempt us to forget momentarily that we are love, and that love is the greatest power in the universe. A universe of love was created by a sequence of small, Divine sparks …of the conscious intent to become far greater THROUGH loving…and that universe of love surrounds each and every one of us right now…even when we cannot, or will not, see or feel it.

It is possible to become attached to just about anything, including 'the struggle' or the way in which we are being asked to serve love… yet, attachment and true inspiration do not sit well together. So let us clarify our intentions to be and to become more loving, to become love, to allow love to move through us, inspire us, show us how to change the world in a way that has lasting impact and remind us that our beautiful universe of love is tireless and bountiful. Yes, we can have most of the things our minds can dream up for us to desire …yet there is always a greater truth that shines beneath our desires and says that whatever else happens…we are love, love is the true creator of all that is meaningful and love moves in perfection!

How to Make Pancakes for the Soul

Something I've wanted to address for quite some time now is some of the peculiar attitudes I've encountered over the past few years in relation the many wondrous and varied healing modalities we have at our disposal. We are so, so very blessed that at every point in our evolution and transition, if we should experience a physical, emotional or psychic discomfort of any kind, Mother/Father/ God/Nature/The Universe finds us a cure. So why do we keep doing that human thing of negating and criticizing some of these tools, when they all serve a purpose and fill a different need at each stage of our journey.

While totally respecting everyone's view on any given healing and personal transformation modality, my heart is bursting to say something, to remind us all that this is, once again, just a calling from the lower mind to dissolve every good thing into the murky waters of conflict and separation. We know in our hearts that whatever path we choose, it is US, our most inspired selves, who are doing the healing…or rather, the Divine Universal Prana, chi, Ki, Divine Consciousness/God that makes up the individual and collective spirit of what we appear to be.

Whatever we might choose to call it, in any given moment, it is working through us, regardless, in order to reveal itself at some point, in its purest and most exalted state, THROUGH the use of whichever modality we choose. Whether we use NLP to dissolve the beliefs that prevent us from knowing, at the level of mentality, that we are God, or use Reiki to strengthen our energetic field so that we will develop a stronger 'knowing' at the soul level or scream until our heads almost fall off so that our hearts can unravel centuries of pain, as we slowing come to love ourselves and remember that the heart is the place of perfect love and not a safe harbor for affliction! Smile!!!

So recently, I began to explore a therapy, which had fascinated me for quite some time and after studying part one of this modality's teachings, I felt satisfied that I had discovered enough for the time being to suit my needs at present. So I decided not to go any further with those particular studies. However, I was surprised at some of the reactions I received when I shared some of my excitement about Theta, and saw the relief expressed by some of my friends that I'd decided not to take these studies any further.

I was so puzzled by these reactions and have since heard all sorts of things said about the therapy and the people who are drawn to it. Yet, every one of the practitioners and friends I met on my own, personal Theta journey were very special people and true beings of loving light.

If you have eggs, milk, flour, buttermilk and spices whipped up in a bowl, the chances are, you'll be able to make some really nice pancakes. If someone comes along and decides to add a horrible amount of lemon so the batter curdles…and someone else adds so much salt it makes your tongue burn and someone else adds water and makes the whole thing a bland old sorry mess, does that mean that the original mix wouldn't have made a great bunch of pancakes…in the right hands!!! With the right consciousness!!

Once again, trust that everything you need for your greatest, deepest healing, everything your heart, soul and spirit need to get you through this somewhat irritating transition into 5thdimensional consciousness and being, already exists somewhere on one of the many different planes of manifestation and everything you need will be brought to you at just the right time in, just the right way and you will gain from it exactly what you need. So add your own spices, find that perfect pinch of salt, chocolate chips…why not!!! And ladle out your loving sustenance with just the perfect dollop of finesse.

This weekend, I was horribly misunderstood for something I said, which was completely misinterpreted and I had to deal with not only feeling horrible about being misrepresented but also in pain about the idea that I might have upset someone. What did I do? After a night of torment, I let it go because I know what's in my heart, I trust it and so does everyone I love. They feel it!!

- Trust what you feel and know what you know!!!
- You are whole and complete
- Trust yourself! Know that none of this is real and try not to take offence
- This is YOUR journey. No one else can walk it
- You will always be the best at being you! Love what that is and listen to it.

- Study ALWAYS improves the mind/heart/soul even if sometimes only by default.
- Do not be static! Keep moving. Keep trying things! Keep learning! You never know where your next great lesson will appear or when your next greatest message will awaken before you in golden ink.
- Open your mind, trust your heart!
- Be excellent to each other!!! (Lol!)

So basically, on the subject of choosing your vehicles for healing, explore! Chances are that if you are firmly on the ascension path, at some point your old 'stuff' will get stirred up and demand that you release it from its absurd little word-wang and become the Divine being that you are!!

At some level, we created our stuff and thankfully, we have also created the cure....both individually and collectively. There are no good guys and bad guys here, just a lot of violence flying around in the general, psychic field, waiting to get exorcised so that we can begin to see the beauty and truth of who we really are. We are all responsible for all of it, the good, the bad, the ugly and the truly beautiful and transcendent!

A world of wonder awaits at the end of this journey and a multitude of Angels even now sing a song of YOUR name, welcoming you home to yourself.... Without judgment! And the truth about how to make pancakes is that ... for you, there's only one way!! Your way!!

Constant to a Dream

Well, it's a couple of days after Valentine's day and the inhabitants of the finer dimensions are "appealing for calm", as this year in particular has seen much violence. Not only as rigid structures in our political and global systems continue to crumble but as relationships are also suddenly revealed for what they truly are and also begin to disintegrate, if built on false premises.

So what's to be done... for the faithful lovers, the spiritual warriors with one foot in the fifth dimension, who understand that the destiny of humanity is to learn unconditional, universal love but who nevertheless long for the touch of the one infinite and perfect love who will show them the mirroring of their infinite perfected selves...the twin flame. Well, as you know, I feel as restless as the world is at this time when I find myself swimming in clichés J and indeed there is not much else to be said on the subject, for those who have been patient for some time and have pored over every possible book, website, video and every other avenue of scrummy twin flame investigation, finding only empty promises manifesting in the day to day reality of their lives.

Those who have now chosen to wait might feel, on some level, that they are being cheated somehow. The rest of the loved-up world drifts happily by, while they remain foolishly constant to a dream. And yet, at some point, regardless of whether or not you accept the twin flame paradigm, at some point in your evolution, something in your soul will cry out NO! No more now. I am waiting for 'the one' and none else will do... if I have to wait forever.

Let us remember, though, that our current path of evolution, by its very nature also relies on us all remaining constant to a dream. We are being called to keep passionately in mind and heart, a reality we cannot yet see, hear, feel or touch in a tangible way, and yet we still believe in it. We have no choice!! Because we know that somewhere in our believing, somewhere along the dreaming way, we create a place where dreams and reality become blurred in definition. So we continue to dream, not knowing for sure whether we are just up to our ears in idealistic madness or true revolutionaries of heart and mind. And then, one day... just when we have forgotten how to say which is which: which is the dreamer and which is the dream; which is the real, and which...the unseen...all at once it ceases to matter...

Here is an excerpt from, *Constant to a Dream*, a very long and rambling poem I suspect I'm still far from completing. Even though we are now at forty pages, I still haven't been given the word that it's time to close the book on it, so to speak. Please enjoy friends. Remember that we are never alone. Keep the faith, let there be peace in your hearts and above all things, let the love around and inside you continue to grow you ...and observe all the things in your life that grow out of love... see how they flourish...throughout the year. Namaste friends...
And ....

yet....

What other thought is this?
Oh common sense, be damned for life!!
How *am* I so bereft of bliss
Yet reaching for your kill-joy knife?!
Oh, human frailty, how so brave
Are you to trespass on this stream?
This buoyant, cataclysmic wave
That should drown out your grisly theme!

I have no time for your bleak thesis
Nothing moves when moving pleases
Sense and reason all at once
They make the brightest heart a dunce
They are the ones who stand and wait
Yet serve in *nothing* truly great
The worthless watchers at the door
When Romes are burning by the score

Abounding of the *spirit* sight
Resounding through the ageless night
This is the arrow that must fly
From all restriction by and by
Oh yes, it's *this* that holds the sway
This is the truth, the life, the way

Be*yond* the veil, out*side* the line

All *out* of sense and *out* of mind

The rock that brings the faster fuels

These tumbled stones and precious jewels

The tinkle, tinkle, little bell of

Michael, Gabe and Raphael

And Uriel (who never shouts)

His hand is moving *all* about

It's in a whisper or a whiff

That travels in through other gifts

Another sense than simple holding

Seeing, smelling, touching, folding

Hear them carried on a sigh

That whispers through the heart from high

And from within and all around

These gentle-natured bells resound

Oh yes it takes a trusting soul

Who is devoid of grasp and hold

Who is prepared to trust and see

The sense that comes so senselessly

Oh, yes, oh yes that's how they roll

These mighty brothers swathed in gold

And if the heart is pure and true

They lean a little closer too

Oh come, oh come, sweet friends of light

For I am ready for this flight

Yes, I am one and all with you

Come check me thorough, check me through

Come take a look, my goose is cooked!

You'll never more be overlooked.

Oh clean my heart, sweet gentle God

And welcome me into thy grace

For one more whiff of that sweet sod

Those humours from the summer place

It's Michael now who comes, sweet soul

We heard your cry; it was well told

Yet what now will tomorrow send

When you are tested once again

You will refute us, words will rend!

Oh how we love our human friends.

And will, unceasing, every way

Although you'll see this very day

Your nature does your truth distress

Not once, not twice, not thrice, but guess

How many doubts you might confess

To any score, I'll answer yes

This many times you will deny

But you will see us by and by

Oh yes, you'll find us ...if *you try*

For even Peter sits here now

And watches over all who rise

And even if the cock should crow

He is the rock, the road, the prize

For that sweet soul has paid the price

Of loving lost in search of sense

And safety of the body fence

That heart-betrayer, hard and dense

And in the end ...he left it thence

And so I say, across the line

This ever WILL be, for all time

We're always knocking at your door

For you are ours and we are yours

This ancient, ever-loving stream

Of Heaven's mind and rapture's cream

Whose god-light rays on ancient reams

As weight of gold and words still clean

Are seldom heard and rarer seen

Between their earth-discoloured seams

The master's all whose loving theme

Might guide this shoal of sleepy bream

The lotus-blossomed, waking Prince

The Mecca-beckoned, thus-come-since

The moon-struck huntress and her gleam

The living, loving Nazarene

The holy, holy, precious flame

The golden: stolen, turned and tamed

The Angel host, the elfin queen

The Goddess/God who waits to wean

The lasting arms on which you lean

This humble, superhuman team

Is always and has ever been

ForEVER constant to a dream...

Be a Place-Holder for Paradise

It is not easy. It never was going to be easy to endure or to observe the changes mother nature insists are necessary in order to bring the world back into balance, back into its true vibrational resonance. Many of us are deeply shocked and feeling great sorrow for everyone who is left behind to mourn those lost in recent catastrophic natural disasters and those who are struggling to pick up the pieces of their lives in the aftermath.

I felt compelled this morning to deliver this message of hope, to light-workers everywhere and my deepest wish is to also pay proper respects and send out prayers of healing and petitions for Angelic comfort to the people of Japan while doing so. Please join me in this and, as always, multiply our intent by doing so. Thank you. It is done.

The world is changing rapidly now. The earth is readjusting itself, the old is hanging on by its grubby, grabby little fingernails, the literal, physical polar shift of the planet is taking place almost before our very eyes and those who thought they held power are beginning to witness true power perhaps for the first time ever. The power of the inevitable realignment of the earth and its inhabitants with God consciousness; divine consciousness; correct, magnetic energetic frequency; remembrance of what we are; re-connection with source; our embodiment of light, creator consciousness, Atlantian and Lemurian society, the garden of Eden, cosmic re-alignment, mass evolution, remembering paradise, Summer 1967...lol. You choose. There are so many beautiful metaphors and possible ways of describing what is taking place all around us, right now, and yet many still do not believe we are witnessing anything particularly extraordinary in spiritual or evolutionary terms.

Even many precious lightworkers are labouring under the unfortunate and disillusioned misunderstanding that other forces are somehow winning, beating us into submission and laughing all the way to the bank. It is NOT so. The NATURAL order is on the home stretch now. The natural, loving order...is in charge now. Not one being who lives breathes, walks or talks, even the most magnificently aligned and inspired channel can begin to anticipate what comes next. There is no current frame of conscious experiential reference for it. It's quite literally mind-blowing. But all are celebrated and applauded for our great courage, faith, prescience in following the light and inner guidance of love, without question and for the love of all great loves: the higher call to loving service that has brought us all to this point.

I can only marvel now at the journeys and the weaving and the twisting turns of the paths of myself and other soul-family light-workers particular over the last year or so. We certainly stepped up!! Invisible, underground warriors, keepers of the flame, trusting in the sense of our seemingly senseless behaviours, I and your unseen Angelic companions love you so.

The following short inspired message came streaming into my mind this morning almost as one sentence, one thought. Peace and deepest gratitude, once again to my guide and precious (ever-patient) friend Peter Elohim for this special message. Love, peace and big hugs to all.

"Be a placeholder for a forgotten paradise. Be a marker and a maker of peace, loving kindness and Divine longing. Place THAT flag in the ground. And when the madness stops, you will be like an archived seed from the first innocent rose, planting your precious roots in renewed old soil, with great care. Hold on!!! Your time IS coming!! Your time is here."

Cluster-Fukushima

Those who are very sensitive to energies are perhaps wondering why there was such a weird heaviness suddenly appearing at the end of last week, building over the weekend and seemingly dispersing over the last 24 hours or so. Please don't worry; it's all just more global, energetic, emotional cleansing as our hearts go out to all those who have transitioned in recent weeks and our energies go out towards lightening the load, regarding the dark energy precipitated by the anti-loving nature of radiation.

Just know that there will be times when our efforts as light-workers will involve all kinds of cleansing methodologies, for which we have volunteered on the inner planes, at the levels of higher consciousness, but of which we might be completely unaware at a conscious level. And in all of our contributions, those in the finer dimensions work with us constantly to amplify our efforts and to ensure that we achieve our aims. Please know, also, that as this particular burst of our clean-up campaign comes to a close...for the time being... we should utilise fully, the many possibilities for self-cleansing available to us... Salt baths are particularly recommended at this time (energetically speaking) because of the peculiar nature of the energy we have been clearing and its tendency to get 'under the skin'. I have been experiencing it as a slow, sticky energy that makes it tricky to think clearly or to feel as sharp as I might like to. It has also been (how can I put it) a MAJOR downer at times. Still, away it goes, at least for a week or so, and tonight I've got an extra-special salt-soak planned with incense burning and maybe Master Choa Kok Sui's beautiful Om chants ringing around my home. That ought to do it... otherwise, I'll have to bring out the big guys. Lol. Please feel free to share your energy-clearing experiences and tips with us here so we can continue to bring the radiance back into our hearts and our surroundings.

There are also several ways we can clear our energies by giving attention to the workings of the physical body....diet, certain forms of exercise and purification etc. I know that many of my lovely soul family of light-workers have been drawn to working in this way recently and this message is for all of us and for all in the human family who may or may not feel as we do but who work with us, nevertheless. There is not one person on earth who does not play a part, not one who is above or below another and in the end, even out of the darkness, comes light ...yes indeed. So, just as the antics of political leaders of recent years, and the banking system in general, have sparked wave after wave of societal questioning (also playing a part, by default, insisting with their unscrupulous behaviour that we begin to demand better for ourselves and our children) perhaps this current disaster should lead us to ask, *whatever happened to the search for clean energy and the idea of properly subsidised research into the true and potentially beneficent power of the universal energy all around us.*??

Neptune's arrival in Pisces (another momentous energetic adjustment to make) should help to quell some of the angry tantrums of Uranus in Aries. My guides are pointing out to me that their recommendation for us, under this beautiful, watery influence is to be extra mindful of the power of all things that flow freely and are not easy to quantify. We should also recognise one of these very powerful transits as a potent force for softening and mitigating the tumultuous effects of the other. In other words, the energy of positive, dreamy, loving intention should stream out from us ...and from the benevolent, universal forces surrounding us...(Neptune in Pisces) to combat the energetic effects of heat, disruption and sudden angry eruptions of radiation (Uranus in Aries)much more easily now...

Love should flow out more effortlessly now, to heal the energy of war and domination, water should be consumed profusely to combat the effects of fire and dehydration, those who have this resource should charge their water with Reiki symbols before drinking, so that this ancient, nebulous means of *shaping energies for the betterment of all* might be used to combat the effects of manipulating energy for destructive means... in other words, nuclear power. Those who don't have this resource could simply pray over their water or set the intention of charging it with love, so that love's mysterious quality might soothe our fiery hearts and remind us all that this is a love revolution we are creating and nothing else will be as loving or as lasting.

Rest and meditate when you need to, and drink deep from the well-spring of love that you surely now know ...truly surrounds you. Then come back to your place in this beautiful evolution-revolution, refreshed and renewed.

So we begin to see the possibilities for our own self-salve-ation, drawn out clearly, as always, in the stars – those constant markers of our potential progress as evolving beings here on earth.

However, I'm not an astrologer; I am as always, just allowing the sweet whisperings from my precious guides to influence my ramblings and to bring to you, in joy and gratitude for this very special work, whatever you need to continue on, precious light-workers...

Love, light, peace to all, from me and from all who reach out to you, *through* me, in love-light consciousness, from the beloved hereafter...

Osama's Dead

♥ *Today, I return my focus to loving, Divine alignment, peace and celebration of difference.*

Today, I hold in my heart, the possibility ...the reality...of infinite, unlimited Love.

I call it into my being now.

Today, I choose to trust in the triumph of love and true understanding, over all illusions...

There will be no dancing in the street.
Today, I choose to remember that all of life is sacred ♥

Part 2

Peter Elohim

Introduction

My Guide had a lot of trouble getting me to write this half of the book. Let's just say I had some resistance to being the kind of person who could write something like this and then claim boldly and confidently that it was in fact not my work but the channelled thoughts and ideas of some other being, some disincarnate spirit. I had up to this point mentioned my guide in most of my messages and books so far. It would have been felt wrong not to, considering the all the help I had received from him. However, once again my faith, courage and belief were to be tested as I wrestled with the idea of allowing him to channel through me without any interference or input from me, whatsoever...

Every time I sat down to begin, I felt the cold, creeping fear of the ego and its nonsense forcing me to suddenly remember some incomplete housework task or some essential email to send or some urgent phone call/distant healing/must-see website/group events schedule/meal (important to eat little and often)! On and on it went, every time I was supposed to put in another stint at the laptop, I became like that restless child in the classroom, always putting my hand up to be granted permission to leave the room under some flimsy pretext and probably ever so slightly frustrating the heck out of my kind and ever-patient teacher.

So although, during the times that we were actually engaged in writing together, my conviction regarding the veracity of Peter's existence was undeniable and unshakable, I just couldn't make that final leap into announcing to the general populace in such a defined way that he was absolutely real and separate from myself.

It was ok when we were alone, so to speak or while I talked enthusiastically about my Guide to fellow Angel-teachers, channels, mediums and other people who totally got it, (some of whom had actually even met him, briefly, themselves). But the problem was with the thought of speaking up loudly and proudly about it when I was suddenly out of an enhanced, 5th dimensional state of awareness and in "mixed company." What would people think of me? Wasn't I already strange enough? Wasn't, refusing endless opportunities to socialise in favour of a lap-top, permanent pyjamas and a long-dead best friend, already leaving me pretty 'out there' on the fringes of society? I really wasn't sure I was prepared to go any further out... I was already in the Greenland of social involvement!! Why couldn't I just keep writing 'fiction,' I loved that...that was easy, and fun!!!

So even though I was being shown another possible way of working which would bring even more love, light and awakening into the world, I still doubted. So, in spite of this wonderful experience and all of the wonderful writing Peter and I have created together, *and* the endless proof and validation which has come from his insightful guidance during my meditations, there I was, still begging for reassurance.

A while ago, I was attending a healing/psychic development circle at my local spiritualist church and I remember on one particular night, our teacher set us an exercise. We were to be led into a guided meditation, and during this journeying visualisation, at some point, we were to find some symbolic image we could bring back for him and, if appropriate, give him a message based around this symbolic object. So off we all went into our beautiful green garden landscapes, obediently emptying our minds to see what would come.

It was a very pleasant meditation, as always, and this time the theme seemed to be food. My guides led me to a place where there were cows standing around in a very rich and verdant field and the sun was shining brightly. There was butter and cheese being churned nearby and bread was baking in the kitchen of a nearby cottage. There were leprechauns leading me off to have a little dance (nothing new for me at all....okay now's not the time to open *that* up).

"Ah," I thought to myself "Obviously my teacher needs to improve his diet and could probably also do with a holiday somewhere very rural. Perhaps he has connections to the countryside ....maybe Ireland...and has been considering a trip recently."

Then just as I was about to return from my lovely journey, I felt a presence interrupting my left-brain interpretations and musings and gently saying, "Oh, yes, and you might want to take this with you," and with that, I was handed a single white rose. When we had all returned from our meditation, our teacher did the usual round robin, asking each of us what our experience had been. And as he listened, our lovely instructor - also a wonderful healer - looked fairly pleased that we'd all had such pleasant journeys but remained mysteriously unimpressed with our offerings. He came to me eventually and I told him all about his diet and his need for a holiday and he accepted it all graciously, with a smile. Then, almost as an afterthought, I told him about the white rose I'd ben given at the very end of my meditation and it was at this point that he raised his eyebrows, gasped, looked very pleased and continued around the room after promising to "come back to that later." I was intrigued!

Once he'd been around the circle he turned to us all and said, "Well, you all had some really nice experiences there and did really well; that was lovely. But some of your guides have been working especially hard on your behalf so we should thank them for that. The reason I say that is that before you started, I asked your guides to give you something specific that you could bring back to me at the send of the meditation. And one of you got it absolutely spot on. We all gasped and stared at each other, each person convinced that they'd struck out as a, now confirmed, psychic numpty, and all pleading with our teacher to tell us what the mysterious object was and get it over with. He paused for effect and said smiling straight at me, "It was a single white rose."

So, okay, the reason I'm telling you that story is not so you'll think... "Ooooh how clever" or whatever. It's just an important part of the journey that got me to finally stop finding mindless tasks to keep me away from Peter Elohim and his further offerings. The white rose experience took place several years ago, now, but has stayed with me and has often reassured me at times when doubt has loomed large on the horizon.

Anyway, a few mornings ago, somewhere in this process of making the leap from inspired writer to channel, my ego was asking for reassurance once again. On this particularly fraught morning, I was resisting to such a degree that even the white rose incident was not serving to quell my fears and once again, I was deeply questioning those inner promptings to write "on behalf of" rather than in a cooperative partnership *with* Peter. Peter was, let's just say, impressing upon me psychically, the urgency he was feeling in wanting to get me back to work. (He doesn't seem to consider making calls, organising printing or thinking deeply about internet marketing to be work). Every time I sat in my morning meditation, I would see him holding a large white leather-bound book and thumbing through its blank pages, kind of, suggestively.

I was again going through a lot of changes with having recently moved to a new home and wanting desperately to get my writing 'out there'. Being back in London was making me feel harassed and there never seemed to be enough hours in the day. How on earth was I supposed to start writing again...? The writing phase was surely over now. Where was all this time supposed to come from?? On and on I wrestled and wriggled until suddenly, the pressure became too much and I just suddenly found myself crying uncontrollably, right there in the middle of my morning meditation I admitted to myself that I was terrified. Well as is often the case with crying (and with meditation), once I had released what was 'really' pre-occupying me, I was free to allow the truth to appear. I was scared and lonely and didn't want to end up being even more alone in "all this". However, I slowly began to relax, as I started to feel the unmistakable presence of Angels all around me, calming me. And then without warning, I gradually became aware of something that was being placed in my hands. As I sat there calming myself and slowing my breathing, a single white rose was handed to me, gently, and I heard a voice saying "believe."

So, I came out of my meditation and decided to once again, open myself up to the writing process, asking the Angels to stay with me, soothing my doubts and fears, throughout! Later on in the day, it was time to have dinner with my daughters. During dinner, the topic of conversation somehow turned to a spontaneous meeting my daughter Rachel and I had once had with one of her guides while I was giving her a reiki treatment. "Oh yeah, I remember that, mum," She said doubtfully. Then after a slightly uncomfortable silence; the kind that often occurs when one of the girls is about to say something they think might be slightly controversial in some way.

"The problem I have with it though, is sometimes it seems so real and then sometimes I don't even know if I believe it...I mean I do believe it ...*kind* of...but, well how do I know if it was really real? Do you know what I mean?" I could hardly believe what I was hearing. I laughed and shook my head in amazement at the intriguing and wonderful way our lovely Angels and Guides often work in order to really get their message across: the wording – almost echoing my thoughts, the unbelievable synchronicity, the perfection in timing and innocent expression. What my daughter, Rachel, was suddenly saying, completely 'out of the blue,' on the very same day of my own crisis of faith, was the perfect mirroring of the doubts and dilemmas I was now struggling to reconcile within myself.

"Hon," I said gently, smiling with rueful wonder, "I've got years of what should be 'proof' behind me, and I still regularly ask myself those very same questions." I then went on to share the story of my current dilemma with her and we all smiled knowingly, noticing how perfect it was that she should bring this up now. But there was still more to come from our non-physical friends.

My girls both have fantastic fashion sense, although they each have their own unique style. That day, as is usually the case, Raiche was wearing a very interesting outfit, a floaty, fluffy white skirt that made her look like a fairy, and a purple top.

Nothing really unusual there but my eye was suddenly drawn to something that she had hung up on the wall upon entering the room utilising a conveniently placed picture-hook. She had removed her main co-ordinating accessory from her outfit and, for no apparent reason, had generously and mysteriously donated it to the general decor of the room. I could vaguely remember having seen it pinned onto her top when she had arrived home a few minutes earlier and thinking how great it looked as a compliment to her white skirt. But it was only then, in the middle of our conversation about failing belief, that I suddenly focussed in on it properly and realised exactly what was...a huge silk white rose...

Needless to say, I shared the rest of this continuing and multi-layered story and began writing in earnest the following day. Since then, I have decided to just sit at my laptop in a slightly altered state, quieten my ego, wait for inspiration...and just see what happens. So, once again, please enjoy the fruits of the poetic, wise and infinitely loving tenure of Peter Elohim.

A Message from Peter

My name is Peter Elohim and I am the patient ever-loving guardian of Diane, the faithful medium who has allowed me, for the purpose of dissemination, to channel through her these few words of hope.

For some time now we have been working together, sometimes with, and at others without the medium's conscious knowledge but always with a sense of ever evolving surprise and lightness. It is my wish at this time to communicate with you directly as there are certain things which need to be said perhaps a little more directly, and in this endeavour, I will attempt to shed some light on what I see as, perhaps, some areas of questioning regarding a number of subjects relating to the matters of the spirit and the changes which are currently upon us all. Blessed be.

Firstly, regarding preparation for the coming changes and the ascension process I will say one or two things which may or may not surprise you. In a sense, they are not so much surprising as perhaps reassuring. Please be assured that you are receiving much help in this preparation and only need to ask for more and it will be given. This is not something with which you need to struggle or something you need do alone. It is your truest nature to be at peace and *our* truest nature to be of loving assistance to you. Simply remember regularly to let go of all concerns and become reunited with that fact. When you feel yourself descending into doubt, remember that help and up-liftment are only a thought and a request away. To focus on the light of a single white candle as you reaffirm your intent to reach to the highest for this succour will, as you have been told many, many times, ensure that this is so. As the changes step up their pace, do not be afraid, for this is every reason for you to become even more hopeful, even more inspired and to lift your hearts even higher, or should I say, more accurately, lighter, toward the finer vibration which is even now, once again reaching out to uplift you.

Remember also that it is not a time or *place* that you are travelling towards, so much as a joyous state of being. And in so much as it is possible for you to gain glimpses of this blissful state even now, if you take the time out of your day, every day, to focus upon your true nature and the true nature of all things, you will find that everything in your life will begin to become more fluid and supple as this awareness begins to grow and to expand into your daily consciousness.

I am not what you might imagine. I am not some other-worldly being who has travelled through many galaxies and dimensions to be with you and to deliver to you some great wisdom from 'on high' which will somehow serve to save and/or enlighten you. For one thing, you simply have no need of saving. There is no trumpet call, no crashing of symbols, no fire-breathing thing descending from on high of which you need be cautious. And secondly, although I have reached a greater level of awareness regarding that which is necessarily in one's awareness as a human being in physical incarnation, I too am nonetheless also on a path towards another kind of enlightenment. And this involves, among other assignments and labours of love, learning more about how to understand, connect with and ultimately communicate coherently with you in the name of the blessed all and all. I am in fact almost identical to you excepting the fact that I am of a much lighter frequency and in this sense, at this current time (in other words as long as you are incarnated fully enough to be wearing the current disguise of human being) I live much closer to, and in more conscious alignment with the heart of that which you call God.

This is of course, a fiercely inaccurate and somewhat limiting description but it will serve us well for the time being. I am your brother/sister and a fellow seeker of that which is most beautiful and sacred. I am also evolving, as do you, through the means of separateness from The One and the desire to be once again re-joined. And I continue to know myself as that which I am, and to revel in coming to know you in your fullness or that which is possible for you to become, beyond that of which you are consciously aware. WE bring you now to the awareness that it is also possible for you to, once again, be reunited with All That Is, to a greater extent, and to once again know me and others of my 'sort' (for want of a better word) as your loving brothers and sisters whilst you remain in full human incarnation, through the great love of the spirit of all that is. There will, indeed, come a time when Angels will walk among you on earth. However, more on this subject later.

You might want to know why this particular channel has been chosen. Suffice it to say that this plan was agreed at some time in the pre-birth stages of her current incarnation and that it has also been honed and reaffirmed through certain lessons and rites of passage, time and time again. It is not so much that the subject was chosen; it was more that the subject was ready. Many, many, many of you have, at this time, been chosen and many of you feel this awareness as a stirring in your souls to do more, to rise to more, to speak out and let your love be shared and heard. And to you we offer this: WE are ready whenever you truly, truly are. Keep on offering yourself, perfecting yourself, checking your motivations and searching your heart and know that we will be doing the same and watching and waiting for you. And when you are ready we will make ourselves known to you. So you can see already what a glorious plan this is. When you are open and clean (or clear) enough to receive this communication, then it will come and so therefore, do you see how we are bringing you up to the light once again in so many, many ways? And yet this is not a test, it is not the dangling carrot, the bribe that says, oh, when you show us that you are a good boy or girl we will deign to come to you and impart this awareness to you. It is simply this; while you are incarnated into a physical body and human consciousness, we, you and I, are from places in *consciousness* which are so diverse that it would seem almost unfathomable that we might ever find a meeting ground. So in order that you might communicate with us, you must literally have a shift in your vibration which will allow our energies and consciousness to form a compatible partnership with yours. Therefore, you must become more like us and we must seek ever to understand you. And this is what brings us together...again. In a sense, there is much within this assertion which encapsulates the meaning of the process of ascension except that there is no limit, as is perhaps suggested by this description. For as you become more like us and more able to form this communication, you might find we suddenly give you a gentle nudge further into the finer vibration, in keeping with the request of your higher being. So do not see ascension as an end in itself, but an opportunity to further grow and become increasingly able to know yourself, and God, as love, with ever evolving certainty.

Likewise, do not be focused on a time and date when it will occur as in doing so, you are partially giving up responsibility. And yet it will come in time, but the time is to some extent still dependent on you and your efforts: efforts of thinking of feeling of picturing and envisioning of reaching up, reaching out, requesting, petitioning; none of this is lost. Through every individual consciousness, there is a golden hand reaching down into each life to guide it onto the golden pathway walked by the many and various masters who have come before to show you the way. And within the consciousness of this planet at this time there is a macrocosmic golden hand waiting to guide you all, as an entire consciousness, into a golden age. It simply takes awareness, acceptance and this continuous reaching up, to allow this dream to come into being. Add to this your loving words, loving thoughts, smiles, acts of kindness, prayers, meditations and your determined and steadfast connection with the higher self and the full light of consciousness, on a daily basis, regardless of the stresses and strains of life.

These are all ways in which you can begin to recognise and allow the God within you to grow and to expand and shine its magnificent light on earth. Follow your truth in each given moment and follow that inner star which is constantly leading you into your own personal and unique way of bringing even more light into this beautiful new time.

At certain points throughout history, myself and the blessed soul now writing these words, have taken to writing and disseminating many 'truths' with which we hoped to enlighten, uplift, teach and educate others for the good of the All. And it is in doing this that we now, once again, find great, great joy. However, we are inclined to express our wish that you take these teachings into your heart only if you can truly accept them as wholesome and useful to you. Either way, it is our sincerest wish that this or something better now serves to bring you a little closer to the light of true consciousness which even now burns within you.

And so, you and I have begun to speak directly, now, on the topics which may be of some concern and I will continue to develop these themes further and to offer ways and means of staying in alignment with the truth of your beloved, blessed soul. Blessed be.

Prayer

The important thing to remember about prayer, in this remarkable time is that prayer is also not what many have been led to believe it is. Prayer is a communication, just as every thought is a communication of sorts, which goes out into the dynamic creative field and begins to set in process some kind of reaction or other. For the purpose of this text, however, let us simply focus on effective ways of praying. There is no right or wrong way to pray, we can only offer at this time a suggested means of prayer and perhaps a few well chosen words which might help you to find and to feel this Divine connection which you seek. If the purpose of prayer is for you at this time, to get out of pain, to get something you want or to 'get' anything, then you might not find these prayers useful. Just know that they are the kind of prayers which will serve their purpose in helping you to feel and know yourself simply as love and the peace which passes and surpasses all understanding, when this is what you are truly desirous of, as you pray.

And this is where we come to the crux of the matter where prayer is concerned. And by now, every seeker of truth must surely understand that true prayers are the prayers which are sent out from the heart; sometimes even without your conscious knowledge. It is said that your father in heaven knows what you wish for even before you have wished it. And the reason for this is that your heart is a primary connecting point between you and that blessed creative force which we may call God for the purposes of these discussions. This is the word which brings the greatest feeling of joy into the heart of the medium and therefore will be the most fitting description upon which we can convey the meaning at this time whilst keeping the channels of communication open. IN fact it is not the word itself but the very concept which fills US with unfathomable peace and joy, and yet, we also understand the very human need for words and at this time are most grateful for them! As long as all are of a common understanding that what we are speaking of is the immense creative force within the universe, a force which is, at its highest expression, simply the love which gives birth to, and connects all things in brotherhood and sisterhood, then we will continue to use this word with your kind permission.

So on the subject of prayer then, there is nothing in the universe which cannot be given unto you but it is imperative that you seek now not to behave as a needy child, constantly choosing to satisfy the whims of the ego, the smaller self, but to expand the awareness out so that one becomes aware of the greater plan at work in all things, for the highest and greatest good, according to the pre-ordained plan for your precious planet or plane or realm. For it is *this* more universal awareness which will bring you to the greatest fulfilment and inner harmony, and ***this*** is what you must learn to pray for if you would be truly happy at this time. For example, you might want to run a successful business and make a lot of money and therefore decide to use cosmic ordering to help you to create the circumstances you desire. And this is all good and well. Only, when that business fails after just one or two years in operation, you might be called into questioning yourself and the wonderful cosmic ordering process. However, do not question these gifts, these skills of abundance and joyful choice, or you ability to use them appropriately. Instead, why not question God about what is right for you and about what will bring about a truer, longer-lasting happiness. So for example you might begin by making use of a prayer such as the one that follows:

Heavenly Father, enrich my life with understanding of your true purpose for me.
Help me to connect with you in constant prayer.
Divine Spirit please bring your guiding hand into my life
So that my highest purpose for this lifetime be fulfilled.
In and through you alone, I find true and lasting peace.
Fill me up with your light so that I become a beacon, shining your love out into the world.
Lead me towards the light of full consciousness.
Lead me in the light, lead me in the light and lead me, ever, in the light.

Light a single white candle for three nights in a row at the same time and say this prayer as you sit in front of the flame and allow its light to create a peaceful glow in a quiet corner of your room or home. Then allow the prayer to lead you into a meditation which consists of simply sitting with your eyes closed in front of the flame and re-affirming silently in your heart and mind or by verbally whispering; "lead me in the light" over and over again. Just do this long enough for you to feel that you have made a sincere connection from your heart. This might come to you as a feeling of subtle changes in your energy field, depending on your level of sensitivity, or perhaps you will feel warmth in your hands or other changes in temperature or you might simply become aware of knowing when the connection has been made and sense when to stop. Rest assured that your Guides, who will be overjoyed by your new style and intent of petitioning, will be there to strengthen your link with 'the Divine within you' and expand on your awareness.

You might find that after praying in this way with true sincerity and a hunger and passion for God rather than for the things you imagine you need, that suddenly you find yourself feeling incredibly clear about what work you should do and what your heart, spirit and soul truly need. It might be something you'd never imagined yourself doing. Or it could be something slightly unusual from which your soul has been hiding out for many years. However, as it slowly comes to light and you find yourself being guided, as you most certainly will, within a couple of years you might realise that you are somehow doing work you love, enjoying your life more than you ever thought possible and somehow having your every need met and your every wish fulfilled without struggle. Trusting in God does not immediately condemn you to a life of poverty, far from it. But it is sometimes necessary to be *prepared* to give up your attachment to everything you once believed you could not live without, in order to learn how to truly live. When we allow this calibre of Heavenly guidance into our lives we are always pleased with the result and the outcome far exceeds anything we could have possibly imagined in advance. God knows us far better than we know ourselves. God is that part of us which was/is there at the beginning and the end of our voyage into the unknown, and whose infinite eyes can see the entire journey and far, far beyond.

God is the wisest part of us, it doesn't want for us to suffer. It doesn't even demand that we are obedient. It simply allows us to make our own choice and to let the chips fall where they may. But when we *choose* to follow God, we find magic, mystery and joy a-plenty and far more accurately and appropriately fulfilled wishes than we could ever dream up ourselves to order from the cosmos.

And yet it is a great blessing that many are now turning towards cosmic ordering. It is a triumph of the understanding of the responsibility of each spirit and the power held within the shapeless formless all and all. And your willingness to accept such tenets shows that, for us, a door has been flung wide open through which we can walk into the stirring of your questioning hearts. However as a refinement, only, of this process, perhaps just run each new order through the Godhead consciousness and see how it truly fits with who you are. Be open to surprise and delight in new discoveries and uncovering of your true self and your real life. Focus on God always and in time the constant prayer, which is the hallmark of those who choose to walk the path of light in the golden time of ascension, will begin to grow and flourish within you and enrich your life in ways you could not possibly, currently imagine.

Always remember that, whatever you may have dreamed up for yourself, God usually has something far better in mind for you. God has a far better scope of imagination, is far better at creating and delivering abundance and however much you claim to love yourself, you can guarantee for certain that God loves you more. Therefore do not be surprised, disgruntled or disappointed if you have a very strong desire for something but it doesn't quite materialise as quickly as you'd like. If you hand it over to God, you might find that although things are not evolving as quickly as you might like, your plan is unfolding in a miraculous way and in the perfect timing to accommodate delightful, unforeseen events filled with serendipity and added potential for previously unimagined joy. Or perhaps something far better will suddenly show you why the first, original plan would have been nowhere near good enough for you.

So yes, of course you should make decisions about what you desire. Put your desires out into the quantum field, trust the process, and trust yourself and your own current wisdom about what might be good for you and your power to manifest it into the realm of form. Use the awesome creative power with which you have been blessed, but always remember to detach from your desires, stay light-hearted and keep those 'must-have' thoughts out of your mind. Learn how to meditate and commit to this practise with regularity and consistency. Learn how to form a personal connection with the God within you and then nurture it with daily practise.

At first this feeling will be almost indistinguishable from your normal state, but with consistent practise, you will begin to have certain feelings, inklings and inclinations. At first you will question these, they might seem quite nebulous in quality and you might be tempted to write them off as moments of hysteria, imagination or fleeting self-delusion. But the more you pay attention to them, the more they will grow and the stronger they will become. Trust the process and continue, *no matter what*. Do not expect to necessarily hear voices, either, but simply open your heart to the light of consciousness and all that needs to be will be. Go into the process each day with the intention to surrender the lower self and the cravings of the ego and the body, and ask simply for divine intercession, direct from God. Go within and sense the energy of your heart and see it filling up with white light. Or simply use the prayer above to lead you into a short meditation and intend that from this moment on your choices will be Divinely inspired and your outcomes Divinely guided.

If a plan or a wish or desire is sticky, slow or just not working out, let go. This is the time to use the prayer above to help you to tune in and connect with the frequency of God and to see what she/he/it says about your plans. If there's no cosmic laughter and you get a warm feeling anywhere in your body, particularly your hands, just be patient, your dream could be on its way.

Love

So what is there to say on this much documented subject that could possibly add anything to that which has been previously expressed? Quite simply, this: If it feels good, really good, Divinely blessed, wonderful and heart-warming, then it is probably love, if it does not, then it is almost certainly something else parading as love, some uninvited imposter. Love is the highest we can reach for within ourselves and as such, it goes way beyond pure emotion. It is the joy of creation itself, *in motion*. If you have ever watched a baby looking up at its mother with complete and utter trust and devotion, you will know what love is. If you have ever watched an artist painting a Tahitian sunset with such passion and awe that he or she would be completely unaware of your voyeuristic presence even if you were to stand beside them and make unhelpful comments while they work, then you now what love is.

And the reason that love is so often linked to creativity and artistic passion is simply this; when we are fully involved in the pursuit of some great artistic moment of expression which takes us way beyond ourselves, we go alone to meet with our God. We become one with that which is sacred within us and which is closest to that which we were at the very dawn of creation which was simply a creative impulse borne out of love and holy curiosity and the blessed eternal creative urge.

And when two people come together in love, it should always be thus if they are to know the true nature of love and become reacquainted with their immortal souls. To say that you love another person is not something to be confused with having karma to work out with a person or simply finding someone from whom we think we can learn or who can give us what we need either emotionally, mentally, materially or practically. Indeed, there is nothing that any of you truly need which can in fact be supplied by another individual. All of your needs are easily met only when you seek to once again join with the eternal and everlasting wellspring of immortal goodness at the centre of your very own dear heart which connects you to your own dear sweet portion of God. And when you are engaged in some service or other which allows others to remember and to reconnect with this awareness for themselves, then you are, well and truly in the presence of love. For love is the seeing within another that which you hold most dear and most sacred and causing them to see this in themselves.

And does this not, now, put the whole concept into some greater context? For now how does it feel when you argue that another should be more like this or more like that or give you more of this or that in order that you can be satisfied? Has it not been said that God is love and that God remembers every hair on your head and is constant in its all-giving-ness and all-loving-ness? If God is love, how, then, can anything which does not behave like God truly call itself love? When someone wants to hold onto your coat tails and keep you close for the purpose of their own sustenance, is this love? God gives you complete freedom to come and go as you please and to be yourself completely, whatever you might choose to become in this completion. God does not *need* you. When you are betrayed by the indiscretions of another and it crushes your soul almost beyond repair, is this love? Is it love from them or love towards them or love towards yourself when you have this response and agree to play within this drama from this perspective; being done to, derided or damaged in some way? Love has no need to be with one who cannot love fully and love does not betray itself.

Therefore, when such dramas occur, do not call them love, call them 'the drama in which I am willing to participate for my own amusement, growth and for the education of my soul.' Your eternal spirit knows far better. Your eternal spirit knows all about love. It feels good, always, whether it is noticed, ignored, betrayed, admired or belittled; it always resides in a place of love and treats itself and others accordingly. If someone is truly beloved to you, you have no wish to strangle them with affection or to take from them anything whatsoever that they feel unwilling or unable to give. You simply go your way in love at all times and this is your private loving mandate from yourself, your higher being and your God, which is love. And therefore, your love is not dependent even on the existence of any other being or. You would continue to be love, to be in love, in the loving vibration and drifting through life on a cloud of magical, nebulous and unseen love in all weathers, at all times, in feast or famine and regardless of whether you are single, married or otherwise-engaged in the pursuit of capturing and keeping love. And love in turn would gladly visit your doorstep, and knowing that it was free to come and go as it pleases, it would most certainly remain.

Therefore, a divine marriage is one in which the love within is honoured far more than either of the individuals involved. And yet by honouring each other unconditionally, they learn more about how much more deeply they are able to allow this love to take them beyond the pettiness of 'self'. In other words, when you argue, if you search your heart and find that the argument is being prolonged by something you have convinced yourself that the object of your affections owes you, simply ask yourself this; "If I truly, truly loved this person from the highest aspect of my being and loved myself equally, what would I do now? What would love do now? What would God do? If I truly believed that I am all I need to be whole and complete and the universe loves and supports me more than I can even imagine, what actions would I truly take now? How would I speak, think and behave if I wanted nothing more from this person in front of me than for them to be truly happy, to know and to love God as much as is possible for them at this time and to feel completely free to be themselves, how would this conversation then sound? What would be the flavour and tone of it?"

At times we see this very scenario playing out and we recognise that there has been much growth and evolvement among certain individuals. And yet it is the anxiety which comes, when one of the parties involved is unwilling to see the situation from this higher aspect, which brings much turmoil for these evolved souls. And this is how we see it; Whenever you are caught up in this gritty and unpleasant misunderstanding of your best intentions, remember first of all that you are attracting this discomfort into your experience either through the need or the pre-ordained agreement to lead this other soul into the light, or perhaps they are simply mirroring back to you an unconscious uncertainty within yourself as to whether you can or are truly ready to consistently live your life at this higher level of understanding and harmony.

Therefore, think on and do not be dismayed, it is just a marker of your progress, an indication of where you are in thinking and a sign that you need to either accept this role of blessed teacher or quickly decide that you deserve better and will perhaps accomplish your teaching in other ways. Relationships are always a tremendous opportunity for growth, and there are times when we learn the most from staying the course, and there are times when we learn the most from simply walking away, choosing something or someone else or some other avenue of self-love and self-exploration. However, love is love wherever you are and whomever you are with and for however long. Therefore, your decisions about where and with whom you choose to spend your time is a question of self-love, which is also of a very high vibration. Do not be a martyr for love. Seek out those who can love you for who you are, and in sharing such love, you will find that your loving capacity will grow exponentially, and this can only be a good thing.

Spiritual Growth

Religion is simply the ego's experience of God, Spiritual Growth is the heart's searching and the soul's satisfaction of it's craving for God.

In a sense when we speak of spiritual growth we use an inaccurate term because in fact there is technically not really any growth of the spirit. The spirit is already the infinite energy which flows throughout the universe as an ever expanding-branch of the endless creativity of the all that is. And so perhaps to say that the soul is expanding would be more accurate. It is constantly expanding its range of understanding and of experience and, in this sense, is becoming more of itself, more of what it is and more of what you truly are. So this is semantics of course because at the same time we can easily recognise that what we mean by spiritual growth is in fact ego growth or, rather, increased understanding at the level of personality which allows increasingly for the expansion of soul and further embodiment of the spirit into growing expression onto the physical plane, and once again, this is the very nature of ascension.

The spirit seeks always to come into physical being and know itself as a separate entity in form, and it was ever thus, since the very beginning when certain elements of the consciousness of God first fell into time and those physical incarnations of The Source, first chose, or perhaps, rather, conceived, 'attracted,' and created the duality agreement; the path of forgetfulness of the ever-lasting spirit, in order to experience itself *as* consciousness and not as simply being, oneness and formlessness. So perhaps, then to be even more pedantic, it would be more enlightened of me to suggest that what we mean by spiritual growth is in fact understanding of the self as an essential spiritual component, which has come into physical being in order to express spirit through form. So spiritual growth is the experience of increasingly letting go and allowing the spirit to come more fully into the life and to once again take over the guidance of this adventure in form... Your spirit does not grow in the same predictable and linear way that you might expect to witness the growth of a child from infancy to adulthood. As the spirit becomes increasingly apparent within the physical being, this light gives the appearance to the casual observer of one who has "grown" spiritually, but this is in fact a fallacy. You are already whole and complete and all that you are was ever contained within you from the very beginning. In fact to some extent this was indeed the dilemma. And so this all-knowing all-containing fully formed essence of God which is you, chose to express itself in different forms so that it could come to know and to love The All as a separate and beautiful thing and come to know itself as separate and glorious in the likeness of that from which it first sprung. Is it not quite beautiful??

So upon the subject of spiritual growth and particularly for those of you who may be asking, "How can we grow more, how can we reach for the highest within ourselves and know the truth" In answer to all of this I will say that the way to grow spiritually is to simply stand still and notice that you are spirit. The way to reach for the highest within yourselves is to stop reaching and once again come to simply know it, and the way to find the truth is to go within and to fearlessly and faithfully listen to it without question.

When we speak about meditation as we often do, it is not so much that we simply want you to be still all the time. WE know that your world is different from our 'world' and yet even in our realm there is never complete stillness. We love and honour you exactly as you are and wish only to offer some easy steps towards this growth of which you speak. And when I say easy, do not misunderstand me for a minute. The easiest way to bring more of your spirit into more of your day to day existence is of course through meditation, but the path of achieving this feat to any large extent has never been easy, and we all here can recognise and indeed attest to that fact. So understand that we are only too clear on the subject of what challenges you might currently face and the ways in which your faith and conviction might be tested.

All ascension guides have, at some point, undergone the process of ascension. In fact, it might surprise you to know that at this time there are even many who work and walk upon your earth in service with the full ascension process far, far behind them in the history of their lifetimes. Is it any wonder then that many of you are thinking now about becoming more of what you are? Many have elected at this time to return to earth in service of humanity for no other purpose than to love more and to serve, and it is beautiful. WE can see them from where we are, shining like little beacons of light all over your blessed and beloved planet and ensuring that an otherwise bumpy ride will be somewhat smoother and more pleasant. So therefore, when these energetic catalysts for ascension appear in your lives, you recognise 'something different' about them, something that makes you want to be more, to become and to do more and you might seek for a while to hide in the glow of their light, shielding yourself from the inevitable encounter with your own magnificence, putting it off for another day.

But make no mistake, this awakening cannot be put off for too long in these vastly changing times. And I tell you, dear friend, there is nothing to fear but the fear of this great meeting itself. Because in that great moment when you finally surrender yourself, your ego, your self-disgusts, and your fears of retribution up to the highest within you, you will know such deep and abiding holy, holy bliss that you will marvel that you ever felt afraid. And each and every time that you have a trigger come into your life, some catalyst, some agent of true change, simply recognise and give thanks for this great moment and then let it go. Be still and listen to the promptings of your heart. Let love reverberate from your very being. Do not seek to contain this feeling, person or being, Let go and know that you, too, are God. Realise in that moment that the need for possessive action comes once again from the ego and that perhaps a few moments of stillness and inaction will lead you to the truth of this encounter. Let that very encounter be the catalyst for your *own* awakening. Do not seek out leaders who will lead you into the dark. They do not need your power if they are connected to the blessed all. Learn from those whose shine brightly, a little more about who *you* are!

There is no need to run from yourself and no reason to hold on to a golden sun that will undoubtedly rise again in the next, new morning. Simply learn to trust, follow and notice a process, a wordless, senseless process, which makes an unreasonable sense inside your heart. And in noticing, follow, and in following, then, continue to notice and let *your* spiritual process take on a life of its own. So that you will one day come to wonder how you ever believed that you might be anything but pure ever-lasting, ever-loving spirit and blessed instruments of God, each one of you, shining your light through dusky times. Blessed be.

Death

It has been said many times for the comfort and the upliftment of the bereaved that death is just a transition, a passing from one world into another, but in truth it is so much more than this. Each time another body or incarnation vehicle is set aside we move into a new way of being, we return to the true essence of who we are and yet we become much more than we were at the start of each successive lifetime. The soul is ever evolving towards the point of realisation of the oneness of all things and its connection and intrinsic belonging to all things.

The spirit recognises that it is already this. So in a sense it is still inaccurate to say that when we die we return to the spirit. In fact it is the level of soul awareness to which we return, in other words one of the many levels of consciousness in which the individual portion of spirit knows itself to be separate and apart from all things but can chose to merge with or to embrace all things to varying degrees depending upon the soul's level of awareness of this infinite possibility. Even in some realms outside of the body, there is a lack of awareness of the endless creative field of The All That Is and the many inherent probabilities implied by its own very limitlessness. Therefore it is important not to imagine that when we die we automatically achieve a state of instant perfection and all-knowing wisdom.

Yes, indeed there is much, much love in these realms; I'm sure those of you who are able to have often felt it. This love is endless, boundless, limitless in its profusion and in the volumes and reams in which it descends even now upon the love-thirsty earth. However, there are many who upon finding themselves without a physical body remain confused, bewildered or entrenched in some old pattern of repeatedly re-playing some out-moded negative emotion in the form of a holographic, soul imprint which remains like a stubborn stain upon a beloved favourite blouse or shirt and refuses to budge even after several runs through a regular 'wash-cycle.'

And yet there are others who know immediately where they are and what they are about and remember almost on arrival how to create the Heaven they desire. So it is important then to remember about the particular experience of the death of each individual that it is not an out-of-the-blue experience, it is to some extent, another created reality. There will undoubtedly be a welcoming party if this is what you are expecting and hoping for. There will of course be a choir of Angels should you feel inclined to allow yourself to see them. And so it is with life, and after all why would you really need to know so much about death when your body is still full of life and your heart still overflowing with the potential for enchantment with all that co-exists here with you within this blessed realm.

If I told you that right now I am standing right beside a human being and impressing my thoughts and my personality into her consciousness and that the day will come when I will stand by her side as real as you could imagine perhaps engaged in some new creative pursuit without the barriers of time space, disparity of dimension, materialised concerns or in fact any of the current encumbrances which prevent us from communicating in the usual ways which are accepted in your realm, you would probably believe me.

But would you believe me if I told you that this could one day happen right here on earth and not just somewhere in some distant far-off hard-earned Heaven sometime way into the future at the end of this well-lived and beautiful life? How would you begin to think, feel, take care of yourselves, those you love and your world if you believed that you would one day walk with Angels by your side, guiding you, keeping you safe showing you how to love more, learn more and become ultimately closer to who you truly are? So begin to prepare, then, for living and not for dying. Shape and mould your world the way that you create and co-create in the finer realms when you are aware and able enough and blessed with Heavenly imagination. Use what you will to bring your desires and your blessed dreams into creative fruition; visualise, sharpen and hone your creation skills, use light, colour, sound, fragrance and texture to create a Heavenly space for all that you wish to see evolving and growing upon your beautiful earth.

Fill your home, your small corner of cosmic perfecting, with beautiful things, wonderful pictures of inspiring scenes, Angels, waterfalls, mountains, smiling people, loving people and happy Buddhas and much, much lightness. You will soon learn how to decide what to keep in your home simply by how it feels or, rather, how it makes *you* feel. How it looks and how it feels will become inseparable from each other and you will want nothing around your which drags on your energy or takes you away from your lightness. For has it not been said that if your very own eye offends you, pluck it out without remorse. Of course there is no need to take this literally, we do not live in such harsh times and even at the start, this was meant to serve only as a figurative reference point and not a literal instruction. (Smiling).

However, it was ever thus, that what you focus your attention on for much of the time, will grow and grow in your experience. This is not some airy fairy concept but a mirror in much slower and more laborious terms of that which takes place within the lighter realms where instant manifestation is commonplace and in fact not even worthy of note. When you learn how to manifest instantly upon the material plane, you will know yourself to be far closer to what you might call Heaven than you might ever have imagined you could be whilst still living and breathing upon this earth.

Therefore if you wish to create a world of beauty, surround yourself with beauty and you will eventually see this reflected back to you. Pray for the beauty and presence of your Guardian Angels and those who work in the light and in love's holy name to bring about peace and the loving changes you wish to see on earth. Play inspiring music and turn off the news and the noise, avert your attention from stories of doom and gloom. Help out wherever you can but pour more energy into the fire of compassion in your heart than into the lust for drama and horror stories of a failing world at its certain end. Yes this is indeed an end, and it is also a glorious, love-filled and joyous beginning....It is whatever you decree it to be according to your deepest wishes.

Therefore prepare for life and not for death, prepare for plenty and not for starvation look for love and not for reasons to hate and seek out only the light. And when you find yourself in darkness ask that you are shown a way to emerge into the light, flaming, sparkling, radiant and God-filled, and so it is ...according to that which you most passionately decree.

How many people do you know who seem to spend an entire lifetime preparing for death? They are no sooner out of school and into some stultifying job than they are already beginning to think about pensions and wills and all of those sensible things. Before they are in their forties their bodies are full of aches and pains and with each complaint focussed upon the uselessness of their already aging body, you can almost see this very bulk compliantly disintegrating a little more.

And are there not many others who live life to the full, never seem to worry or complain about ageing, feeling tired or not having any security for their old age and then somehow, old age just never seems to find them. Perhaps they do work they love or spend months at a time travelling the world and being touched, moved and enlightened by seeing other scenes and settings and embracing the way of life of those from other cultures. Perhaps they smile more and attract more good fortune into their lives with their simple expectation that all of their needs will be well met as long as their hearts are in good shape both emotionally and then consequently physiologically.

Which one of these people needs and deserves a Heaven more? Neither. But which one is creating one?

So I tell you this dear, dear friends, it is not so much in your searching for all of the answers about death and what happens to you when you die that you find peace and lasting happiness. Even if you are grieving, the most loving thing you can do for the loved ones you may have lost is to keep their memory alive as a joyous song in your hearts and live on fearlessly, happily and always with your mind on the Heaven you can create right here on earth, in preparation for their blessed return in some form or other at some future time.

That which is lost is never truly lost and right now, even at this very moment you are surrounded by a veritable entourage of Angels, loved ones and Ascended beings, all holding within their hearts a deep and abiding love and concern for your individual heart and the future of your beloved planet.

What seems like an end is simply the end of an era and what looks like death *is* as you know, merely the birthing of a new time. And what looks like simply life is in fact an opportunity for boundless resurrection of the eternal song of the heart that beats within each and every being which has ever graced this blessed earth with its beloved presence. Blessed be.

Service

When we speak of service we must immediately remove from this notion the element of selfless sacrifice for that which is offered lovingly, freely and generously from the heart and soul is returned to the giver one hundredfold. Service to The One is also service to the self, service to another is service to The One, service to humanity is service to the self as all beings are connected and service for its own sake with no thought of reward shifts the vibration to a level where one is in perfect alignment with truth; the truth of who we are.

Service releases karma quickly, efficiently and more effectively than a month of unbroken hail Marys or any other such pleas and entreaties cried vainly and selfishly to a God, an ascended being or any other duly appointed deity who, in fact, only truly understands love. Karma is simply balance. In this process, there is no hiding place in which you can hide from yourself. Therefore, although the concept of selflessness can at times become vain and self-defeating, true acts of service, also, cannot be committed from a place of self-interest. There is no reward waiting in Heaven for those who do just works. The reward is waiting now, in this moment, within your own, dear heart.

The reward is in *truly* coming to know yourself as love and the loving expression of your holy father/mother who lives within the all...of which you are a blessed part.

We cannot stress enough this continuum and the interconnectedness of all things, all beings, all worlds. Every thought, every act, every choice has a consequence. And loving service, even when performed at first for selfish or self-serving reasons can, at times, have a way of transforming your consciousness nevertheless. Therefore do not think that some casual act of charity will win you a place in Heaven, rather wish to immerse yourself completely in some beautiful endeavour because your heart simply calls you to it and to know yourself as the vibrant, loving and charitable being who recognises that within every act of Divine giving and Divine grace, there lies the seed of true remembrance of that which you truly are...which is love. Therefore save your prayers if they are not offered sincerely from the heart, and give generously without thought of buying your way into Heaven. Instead, let your entire life become a constant prayer of joyous, loving service.

I have already mentioned at some point, in some earlier work, the peculiar phenomenon which occurs when those who commit to a spiritual way of life and to work which satisfies the spirit and enriches the lives of others seem to be strangely taken care of. How many times have you, yourself, noticed that as soon as a person decides to take up the glorious challenge of stepping into their blessed life purpose, when this purpose involves serving the spirit in some way, they seem to suddenly begin to live a charmed life. Admittedly, this is not always the case, as some have such a heavy burden of karma which they have bravely elected to release in this lifetime and it can seem as if, however many good deeds they perform, their lives almost appear to be somehow cursed. The difference between these two souls can be almost so clearly defined as to lead one to ask, "Why are some people so unlucky and others so apparently blessed when they begin to work in service?" There is of course no simple answer as each example is different. Suffice it to say that when you begin this blessed work of approaching the truth of your life, and setting out to find and follow your true north, as it were, you will gradually be called into clearing along the way, all that stands between you and this infinite truth. However, let us look at the magical syndrome which occurs when you commit to spiritual work and work in service to humanity.

On the surface of things, it might seem as if, when you decide to follow a spiritual path, God and The Angels suddenly begin to look upon you somewhat more favourably and to allow miracles to suddenly begin to appear in your lives. Yes, of course there is an element of truth in this, except to say that it is not *we* who suddenly, somehow, change our agenda, we are indeed, always here, with our loving premise whether you decide to accept us...or it... or not. It is *you* who suddenly become more able to hear our guidance. And this guidance will always in one form or another, eventually, lead you to your highest good, your greatest knowing of truth and your most abundant and joyful existence. Our agenda, if you will, always remains the same; to love and to cherish you till death or life do us reunite, and beyond this, into through and out of as many lifetimes as your sweet soul requires for its own fulfilment. It is also true that when you begin your journey upon the 'right', path... that which your highest aspect has elected at the beginning of this lifetime, the universe begins to recognise that you are in alignment and begins to flow with you.

You might also find that you are suddenly asking us constantly for help instead of turning away from us in shame as you endeavour to blindly seek and follow the promptings of the ego. And as you may already know, the more you ask for our help, the more help we are able to offer. However, if we look more deeply into this phenomenon, we can begin to appreciate that there are many, many factors at play. And perhaps the most important of these is the simple fact that service is an expression of the highest vibration, which is love. It is the physical manifestation of the intention to be, to become, and to channel love through physical means, acts and deeds. And as we know, it is absolutely essential that as conscious creators of your own reality, what each individual needs to do in order to be in the most powerful state for creating and manifestation, is to somehow achieve a more powerful state of focus and to be in the highest vibrational state that one can possibly achieve. And love, fulfils both of these specifications.

Has it not been said that the world was created with love and untold universes with a song, cried sincerely from the heart of some loving being. Embrace fully your loving selves, your loving state and your genuine intent to do some good. They are what shall become the saving of you. For as you attune increasingly to that higher frequency of love, you will find more and more that all around you, little miracles of love are beginning to take place , with or without your prior planning or conscious desire for them. And in time it will be said that love created this world, and in the end it was *love* that saved it.

Upon your planet at this time, there is a wellspring of love surging, growing, springing up from the hearts of the many, many light workers and channels who seem to be appearing in droves all around you and yet you are also one of them. You too, are coming into that blessed state of reawakening which is the unstoppable realisation of all that you are. And as you begin to feel this impulse growing increasingly stronger within you, you might also find that you are feeling the desire to pass on what you have learnt, seen, experienced and understood, to others who might seem baffled by what is currently occurring.

Do not think that service means that you are now expected to travel to some remote land and, sacrificing all that you hold dear, join some great cause and declare yourself to be one who wishes to 'make a difference.' No such proclamation is required, for this may or may not be the path decreed for you. Yet never let the simplicity of your life or the seemingly small acts you are able to perform, deter your from your cause. For I tell you now, each single one of you is right now, even now with the very thoughts you might now be thinking in response to what you are reading, yes even in this moment, you are making a difference.

So what does service mean to you? To us it seems quite clear alright! Service is offered in keeping your thoughts clear and positive, and at all times, leaning your ear towards the lighter, the more positive inclinations in what you choose to absorb from the glut of information around you. Service is in a smile that reminds someone else of love and brings them immediately back up and into that higher frequency with you. Service is in comforting and consoling another light worker who is experiencing the same sensitivities and confusion with which you, yourself, were so overwhelmed just a few short months ago and letting them know that it works out well in the end, and yes, bringing them back up into that higher frequency of love, optimism and light. Service to one, even one soul, is service to the whole, service to the light is a reminder to love and anything which causes another to remember to love has increased your own capacity to love and to become the embodiment of love and on and on it goes until one day you suddenly find yourself in the midst of a deep understanding of yourself as an immediate conscious creator, for as we have said, it is love which creates, it was love which our father/mother (love) used to create the Heavens and the earth, and it is love which allows you to now suddenly feel that your are being rewarded for turning to the light.

It is not a reward, it is simply a return to love, a return to your original blessed state as the embodiment of love and therefore, a remembrance of your own greatest and second most beloved gift which is that of a conscious co-creator in the image of our father itself.

In the process of ascension, somewhere along the way, there is the experience of what many describe as being *in flow*; that blessed state where everything falls into place naturally and easily and your know all at once without a doubt that you are travelling the right road in the right way and with the right companions for the journey. In our realm this is commonplace. That which is out of flow is not possible, it cannot exist because we are in the process of creating all that flows, constantly and there is much, much love and as a consequence there are many, many miracles, and this is your birthright. And our purpose is to facilitate your coming into alignment once again, on a daily basis, with all that flows through your loving hearts from the source of all infinite creation. And this is the meaning of service. Blessed Be.

Blessed are the Pure in Heart

Heavenly father/mother, blessed Angels of
loving light

We are one

One heart, one soul, one spirit

I am in you as you are in me

And only this love is real

Raise my heart, lift my consciousness

To that place where I and my father are one

Bring that love into this earthly vessel

Awaken me to the highest within

In love's holy and sacred name

Freedom

There is on your planet at this time, a quest for freedom at all costs. All around you we see evidence of an increasingly tight stranglehold of the powers-that-be, over the wishes, minds, lives and even the activities of the populous. It is sometimes challenging to watch. But who are these mysterious 'powers-that-be?' Who are these bold enslavers and what do they represent? Well to begin with, if we all recognise ourselves as conscious creators of our own reality, we have to ask ourselves the question; how is this current creation of ours serving us right now in this moment, this nugget of time-space reality consciousness?

Well for one thing, as a result of these violations of freedom, you are now much more aware of yourselves as freedom-loving beings. For another, many of you are now looking for ways of separating yourselves away from those who would seek to do this and those who would allow this to be done. And in a sense, you are, without a doubt preparing to identify yourselves, once and for all as *this*, and not that or as *that*, and not this, and it was ever thus since the beginning of time. So what is so very different about this polarised duality now? Well for one thing, we are no longer at a point in human history where all of the people can be fooled all of the time. And believe me there have been many who have succeeded in achieving this feat of deception throughout this chequered history; time and time again it has been done; in the name of God, in the name of truth, justice, honour, pride, religion even blood. And what is so surprising to us now and a joy to behold is that there is no longer any way that this can ever happen again.

There are even now murmurings, stirrings among the disgruntled and weary who nonetheless seek to keep themselves optimistic in outlook but wide-eyed and incisive in vision, and there is much afoot in these quarters which will soon shock and amaze even the most hard-bitten and cynical among you. For even in the upper echelons of society, even as you read this now, there are Angels wandering through the corridors of power. Therefore, let us remind you once again, when you question your freedoms and witness the apparent whittling away of your autonomy as a free being, you are, right now, freer than you have ever been at any other time in history, because you are now in the process of becoming aware of your power, your freedom to create any story you wish to create within the drama which is currently unfolding.

Do not give your power away once again by complaining and moaning and yet silently falling in line when later questioned further. Simply know that if you hold the awareness of being free, you are suddenly free once again, and if you choose to hold the awareness of yourself as someone who is enslaved, then you, yourself will be enslaving your own mind and ultimately, accepting whatever comes to you from the outside, as a forgone conclusion. The way of things, an inevitable consequence of life on earth; when in fact, it is simply the inevitable consequence of spending a lifetime wandering aimlessly through someone else's dream. Open your eyes!

So, on the subject of freedom, let us now embrace its polarity, which is perhaps the feeling of restriction or duty. Many times you speak of feeling duty "bound" as if duty were another form of enslavement. But hear these words clearly; do not let your hunger for freedom release you from your duties in an unguarded moment; there are always those who still need and depend upon your guidance and care, and it is often at times when we are most restricted that we learn what is of most value to us and what ultimately, truly sets us free...loving service.

There are times when you will want to run and hide away from all of this 'madness' only to find that the madness is in fact everywhere. There are times when it is hard to know when the best thing you could do is to dig your heels in and refuse to move, or to behave in a manner which is rash and unhelpful. Do not be reactive. At times you will indeed need to retreat, rest, recuperate and recharge yourself and your energies, and there is no way that we would ever suggest you simply tough it out when riding the wave of all of these new and intriguing energies becomes too much for you. But we would certainly suggest that going within, is the way to find the peace you seek and turning inwards is the place to which you must retreat if you are to find the wisdom, comfort and reassurance you seek. Continue this practice consistently; when necessary, go within for comfort as regularly as you would go to the tap for water. You do not need a schedule to meet with your God; we are well past that stage now. Go within whenever the need arises and keep on with this silent quest for salvation until one day you simply come face to face with your Blessed Creator and find yourself right in the thick of the almighty well-spring of safety and love which resides within your ever-loving heart.

Yet do not allow yourself to be cast out, exiled or set apart completely from society. Keep a brave and positive outlook and face each new day with renewed vigour bringing your newly discovered peace with you. Continue to touch the lives of others with the simple fact of your beautiful being. If you run and hide or abandon your duty, which is after all, to serve, then you have indeed had your freedom taken away while those who depend on you simply stood by helplessly and watched.

Therefore on the subject of freedom, simply remember if you feel enslaved, ensnared or otherwise disenfranchised, that it is all an illusion!! Stand strong and remember that it is not a reality or, simply, 'the way of things'. Go within and choose the reality of your preference and remove your energy from this one. Seek out like-minded individuals who share you understanding and continue to build upon the amassed consciousness of the many light workers now playing their part in this blessed new evolutionary leap. Continue to focus on your own God-Given right to choose your reality, including the part you play in your own liberation or your own confinement, and continue to choose according to the highest wishes of your dear, dear heart at this time; for this is the meaning of free-will, and yes, *that* is the true meaning of freedom. Blessed be.

Food

Nourish your body with love first and foremost. Nourish the soul and the spirit, and the body will be nourished in kind. For what does it profit the cells of the body if you have filled it with what you would call righteous and healthy foods when they are not gathered, prepared and viewed with love? With just a touch, no, even a thought, anything can become a medicine and a healing for the soul when prepared with love, and even the healthiest of foods can become a poison. So watch what you think before you eat and watch what you eat when your heart is not in alignment with your highest truth, which is love.

Bless everything that enters your mouth, with gratitude, with patience, with kindness and with the sincere desire to be well and to prosper in the heart. Do not rush to eat and if you must, then do so consciously, conscious of love always. Do not argue over your food, and do not wonder where the next meal is coming from. Trust and you shall be filled, ask and you shall receive but worry, fret and confound yourself with fear and your hunger will be insatiable for, in truth, it is not food which nourishes the body, but love.

And has it not been said that your bodies and every living thing with which you feed them are nothing more than space and water? How then can you be nourished by only space and water? How can you be sustained by any living thing when the hunger of the spirit is overlooked? When you do not breathe well, when you do not sit in the silence and wait for word from your God, whichever God that may be, how can you then be fulfilled? When you starve yourselves of the food of the spirit, you will run to the cupboard, time and time again and not find anything that will sustain you. Because your sustenance comes not from that which you eat but from that which is put into that which you eat from the dynamic everlasting field of consciousness around you.

And when you eat of the fruits which have been grown with love and ripened in the sun and cared for with right thinking, you feel this vibration, and it is sweeter fruit than anything you have tasted or known before. And when you ask for a moment, "Why does this taste so sweet?" you are misunderstanding once again and missing the point. The energy of everything around you, everything in your life either resonates with you because it is of like vibration or requires, of you that you rise a little higher, or asks of you that you heal it with your love.

And so it is with your food. Therefore, before you eat, bring your food up into alignment with that which you must be. Show gratitude for it, praise the one who has prepared it, give thanks for the moment when you are able to bring each blessed morsel to your waiting lips, and savour each wonderful moment. For, a meagre morsel of dry bread can become a feast in the hands of a sage. So it was with Moses who was able to feed the multitudes in the desert by drawing in sustenance from the very air around, which is in itself food for the soul. And so it was also with the Beloved Master Jesus who manifested so much out of so very little, with a generous application of love and the simple breath of gratitude. Therefore, when you eat, seek not to be filled up, but to become truly satisfied. Blessed be.

Dearest Lightworkers,

Thank you for sharing your time with us. We are filled with gratitude and love for you, for allowing us to join you in this place of service to The One, at your time of awakening.

We wish you much love, peace and joy as you begin to witness the many miracles you are about to see appearing all around you, taking apart all of your old structures and systems in the times to come.

It will amaze and astound you how many of your 'kind' are occupying positions of power and, in time, they will begin to reveal themselves in full force, drawing new lines in the sands of your timelines and changing the view and shape of your world exponentially... as will you, also, as you add your voices and free will choices to this glorious mandate and finally become 'the powers that be.' Even those who have stolen your language, will be forced to give it back, as you begin to create your own New World, in the image of love.

And yet, beloved light-workers, this will not be the greatest miracle you will witness in your time. The greatest miracle...is and always was...you!

Blessings, love and peace to you as we leave you with a story...

The Appointment

There was once a man who frequently climbed mountains in search of God. He'd been told He could be found at the very peaks of the highest mountains. He'd been told that perhaps in the very act of climbing itself, one could find God, because if this magnificent and all-powerful being somehow happened to be looking down from the sky as you climbed and saw you struggling, he would be certain to reward your efforts by coming to meet you half way. Then he would help you up onto a cloud and sit talking with you until the sun rose, or perhaps just until such a time as you both began to feel that you had talked enough, if ever such a time would come. Or you would die of exhaustion on the way up the mountain and your unfortunate fate would naturally bring you to God.

The man thought about this last possibility. He didn't particularly want to have to die in order to see God, although he wasn't afraid of death. He'd often thought how proud God must be of his courage and his daring. In pursuit of God, he had climbed several mountains but he had never found Him on any of them. After a while, he grew tired of climbing and of the disillusionment he felt each time God failed to show up as expected, somewhere on the mountain trail or at its very peak, perhaps springing up joyfully before him as he sat contemplating the serenity of the desolate landscape.

One day, our man began to prepare himself for one last climb. He was just packing his vital supplies for the trip when he heard a small voice calling out to him from somewhere just below his window. He wandered over and sleepily poked his head out to see who was calling him. But when he looked down, and along the quiet street, he saw nothing.

He returned to his packing and dismissed what he had heard, as imagination…until, all at once, he heard what sounded like hundreds of seagulls flying overhead. He shuddered inexplicably; they too seemed to be calling him over to the window, once again, but why?

Once again, he found himself peering out across the rooftops and hills of the quiet little village he called home. There was nothing remarkable to see at all. He had heard strange stories about how God would sometimes speak to people through birds and other creatures and he was anxious not to miss any messages from Him…after all, hadn't he waited long enough to hear one?

Once again the man walked away from the window and returned to his preparations for the long skyward trek and once again, he heard a strange small voice calling out to him. This time there was no denying it. This time, he ran to his window, but once again, there was no-one there: just a couple of children playing with a ball and calling out to each-other as they played. *Someone is playing silly games with me,* he said to himself. *I don't have time for all this! How am I ever going to meet God if I sit here paying attention to every little sound the wind wishes to make? Who knows, perhaps the neighborhood children are deliberately trying to distract me. I'm sure they would be only too happy to see me become side-tracked by their silly antics and miss out on the possibility of an appointment with God.*

The man finished his packing and set out on his expedition. Perhaps this little trek would be his last; perhaps this would be the one that would kill him. Then there would be no more questions or doubts. And if God wanted to speak to him, he could speak to him any time he saw fit to grace him with his presence in Heaven.

The trek was long and arduous, the back pack filled with supplies seemed heavier than usual and the man soon grew tired and weak. When he eventually reached the summit of the small mountain, he collapsed in a heap and fell into a deep sleep. For a few minutes, he thought he might be dying. But he was awoken suddenly, by a tap on the shoulder from a kindly-looking man who sat calmly in front of him.

"Good evening," he said, wrapping a thick blanket tightly around his shoulders and offering another to the exhausted climber.

"Hello…" The man was puzzled. What was another person doing up here with him? How had he gotten there? Where were his vital supplies? And why wasn't he cold, sitting there in a thin robe and what looked like flip flops, with nothing but a blanket for covering.

"Who are you?" he asked quietly, his lips trembling slightly from the cold. "And what are you doing up here?"

"I might ask you the same thing…" announced the strange visitor. "But that would be silly of me when I know jolly well who you are. Don't you know who I am?"
The climber laughed out loud. "Don't tell me you're God" he said. "That's funny."

"Yes it is, isn't it?" said God, happily joining in with the laughter… "But why is it funny?" God seemed genuinely confused now, but happy.

"I don't know" said the man... "You're just not what I expected, that's all. I mean God isn't …like….well, like a real person… It's more, well kind of a metaphor… Isn't it?"

"Wow, you came a long way to meet a metaphor, didn't you?" said God, twinkling with general hilarity and mischief. "And what of all this talk of things being real or unreal…what does it mean? If you like, I could make myself a little more unreal for you. Would you prefer that?"

God was seemed concerned that the man should have the God he wanted. The man suddenly felt flustered. Was he really telling God what to do? What to be? What was he even thinking? This was all too much! After all, God, if it did exist… had to be something…or someone. Ugh, it was too confusing…
"N…no…." he said, nervously… "It's okay; you can be anything…I mean…anyone…any…..um..."

"It's OK" said God, "let's just go with this model for now shall we? I kind of like the robe. So you got my message then?" He continued, smiling expectantly.

"What message?" The man was still getting used to the idea that God had even turned up, so the thought of getting messages from Him as well was almost too much to contemplate.

"I just dropped by to let you know I was going to be a bit late, and to ask you to wait for me."

"Oh…" said the man, "…yes I did hear something, I just didn't know it was you."

"Ah…" said God… "I thought you looked confused.

"You mean the voice I heard calling me, right?"

"Yeah, that was me…" said God.

"…and the Seagulls…?"

"Guilty…" God said, holding up both hands and smiling sheepishly.

"The neighborhood kids?" he added, shaking his head and grinning incredulously. It all made a weird kind of sense now.

"My bad" said God, smiling good-naturedly…

"So hold on a minute. If those things were all you….coming to see me ….to say, 'I'm going to be a little bit late, please wait for me…' what was the point of all the messages? Why didn't you just come and see me instead. You wouldn't have had to stay long if you were busy."

God shook his head and stared at the man, slightly bewildered…"But you said you wanted to meet me up here!!

Man! Make your mind up! You always come up here to meet me and I never quite understand why but I decided, OK, I'll go with it, it's the way he likes it…I'll go up to the mountain to meet him."

The man couldn't believe his ears… "So how come you never turned up then?"

"I always came…It just takes me a while to get here sometimes, or maybe I'm busy finishing up some stuff and I like to wait till I can give you my undivided attention …and you can give me yours. But I always send a message to let you know I'm going to be a bit late. I mean hey, I try to be everywhere at once but if you insist on coming up to the top of a mountain to find me…it's gonna take me a little bit longer to get here OK?! The least you could do is keep waiting! You get to the top of a mountain to see someone, they're not there right away so you turn right around and come straight back down without even giving them a chance to get there! What's that about? Why bother coming in the first place…?"

"Wow, I never thought of it like that" said the man, just a bit dubiously now…God seemed kind of frustrated with him…God didn't get frustrated, did he? It had never occurred to him that God might have actually wanted to speak to him, might have actually been trying to get to all these appointments and that he just might not have given him enough time to get to them. He thought God had been ignoring him, but now he came to really think about it, that didn't make any sense either.

"I'm really sorry." He said, after giving it some thought. "I'm sorry I made you come all this way and I'm sorry I was so impatient…before." "That's OK" said God, I think we understand each-other a little bit better now, so it's been worth the trip." The man sighed contentedly and sat staring out at the wonderful red-golden sunset. He suddenly didn't feel the need to say an awful lot more. "I'm really glad you came," he said, smiling happily. "Me too…" said God. They both sat together for a while, just like that, smiling and basking in the joy of each-other's presence and the beauty of the golden silence.

"Come and see me at home some time…" God continued after a while. "I think it's only fair that you return the visit now. Anyway, it's much easier for you to get to my place than for me to come all the way up here."

"So where do you live then?" the man asked, wondering if he was suddenly going to have to address decades of religious rebellion and start appearing at his local church on Sundays. God laughed again and shook his head. He slowly approached the man and stretched out a golden hand towards his chest. The man shivered as he felt something warm swirling around inside his heart and then sweeping up and down his body; a kind of energy that filled him up from top to bottom and made him feel as if his entire being was radiating with an intense golden light. The strange hand of light reached in gently and took hold of the man's heart. "This is where I live," God said… "You've gone such a long way to find me somewhere else, when I was right here all the time! And now we've both come a long way to find each-other, haven't we?" He smiled and patted the man's hand as wave after wave of blissful emotion swept through him. And as the sunset slowly turned itself into a soft indigo blanket covered with stars, the mysterious, golden being disappeared inside the man's heart and continued to shine out into the world through his smile.

On his way back down from the mountain, the next day, the man was elated. He had finally met God and realized, all at once that he was God because God was inside him. And all of the years of searching had simply led him right back inside himself, to the centre of his own being. But he missed the God he'd just met on the mountain, even though he now contained it within his heart.

He liked talking to God as a separate person. He enjoyed being able to see what was most beautiful in himself reflected back to him on the outside, through another being. One who could sit with him, talk with him, make fun of him and even make him laugh at himself and discover new things about life.

He thought about God a lot as he felt that peculiar golden flame burning inside him. And on his way down, it was as if he was seeing everything for the first time, as he suddenly began to perceive that same strange, warm, golden light radiating out from everything around him.

The birds had it inside them, the trees did, the whistling of the wind even seemed to speak of it, the sky, the sea, the very ground upon which he walked, and even those pesky neighborhood children seemed to have it burning inside them if he looked carefully.

Soon after his encounter with God, the man lost his appetite for climbing and chose, instead, to take a daily voyage inside himself, to seek out the universe ...in the silent summit of his soul.

We Leave You With a Quiet Smile...

♥ And so we leave you now with a simple thought...

Look for love, follow and trust the light within, expand and grow it and let *this* be your focussed intent for every day of this precious lifetime...it will show you the way out of this confusion and lead us all into a brighter day.

Call upon us often...we are everywhere and within all things and we LOVE you dearly...

Peter and the Ascended and Angelic ones

Namaste All. ♥

Printed in Great Britain
by Amazon